⤜ THE ⤛

MERLIN FACTOR

THE
MERLIN FACTOR
KEYS TO THE CORPORATE KINGDOM

CHARLES E. SMITH

KAIROS PRODUCTIONS
McLEAN, VIRGINIA

Copies may be ordered by phone or fax from Kairos Productions at (800) 711-1569.

The text and folios of this book were set in both roman and italic versions of Weiss. Chapter titles and subheads were set in Matrix. Running heads were set in Gill Sans. Additional flourishes were set in Woodtype ornaments 2.

Cover and Text Design by Kimberly Pollock, Lomangino Studio, Inc., Washington, D.C.

Library of Congress Catalog Card Number 95-078700
ISBN 0-9647687-0-4

Printed in the United States of America
First Edition

CONTENTS

ACKNOWLEDGMENTS

I owe parts of this book to the example, teaching, and inspiration of my teachers, clients, and heroes.

I dedicate this book to Thomas Jefferson and Herman Melville, whose fierce devotion to freedom underscores its purpose.

I am grateful as well to

- Kathy Smith, my wife, for assuring that what I say is genuine and for her creative contributions
- my daughters and sons, for the true test
- Tony Turnbull, for his partnership and for helping me to see which parts of our cathedral needed finishing
- Bill Spencer, for introducing me to a context in which differences can really be resolved
- Dick Beckhard, for teaching me strategy as politics and an orderly approach to development
- Robert ("Bart") Barthelemy, for showing me that flying as fast as thought itself was more than an idea
- Lou Savary, for helping with the initial thinking and structuring of the book
- Malcolm Carson, for offering his courage and honest criticism
- Erving Polster, for helping me imagine an organization that poetically fuses intellect and emotion
- Barry Oshry, for defining the experience of systems thinking and reminding me that my point of view is but one of many
- Ross LewAllen, for letting me see that the truth is more important than money
- Ron Bynum, for showing that fun and innocent purpose stand with grace in the face of disagreement
- Lew Epstein, for demonstrating the priceless value of genuine listening
- Deborah C. Fort, for guiding me with her natural and articulate editing

My deep appreciation goes as well to Penny Blankenship, Barbara Neilson, and Jane Reilly, whose devotion, hard work, and accuracy made this book possible.

I also acknowledge my grandfather Julius Levy, whose constancy of purpose was my earliest experience of Arthurian excellence.

To those I have not mentioned, I ask forgiveness and offer the same.

Charles E. Smith, Ph.D.
Director
Taos Laboratories
1995

INTRODUCTION

The legend of King Arthur and the knights of the Round Table has had mystical appeal for almost 1,500 years. The historical Arthur, a Celtic chieftain, lived in Wales in the sixth century, was mortally wounded in the battle of Camlan, and was taken to Glastonbury, where he died. This figure, who flourished during a time of tremendous struggle for the domination of society between Britain and invading Saxon tribes and their allies gradually evolved into the legendary king. The literature he and his knights and the Round Table inspired seems to be without beginning or end.

With a group of the 28 chivalrous knights of the Round Table, Arthur led a quest for the Holy Grail, eventually recovering it and uniting the kingdom. Tales of Camelot, the quest for the Holy Grail, the fellowship of knights bound together in an oath of chivalry, and the great sword Excalibur that Arthur alone could pull from the stone in which it had been magically embedded delight children and invite adults to imagine possibility and magic, as they remember a time when knowledge, commitment, truth, and healing guided lives. People of all ages try to recreate that atmosphere.

On one level *The Merlin Factor: Keys to the Corporate Kingdom* sets forth principles about how to lead an organization into a culture change. The Arthurian myths illuminate simple, useful attitudes and practices that work today as well as they did in the legends. In the fable, Merlin, the king's mentor and teacher, was devoted to Arthur's success and development, both as leader and as human being. A commitment such as Merlin's to another's success and development is the cornerstone of successful and satisfying change for individuals and organizations alike. This book aims to open eyes to see what may be missing in an organization, in its purpose, and in its leadership.

It also indicates, through anecdote and example,[1] how the Merlin Factor can help businesses best fulfill their potential through attention to the two spheres that, when combined harmoniously, make up Camelot. The ancient

---

[1]The identities of all corporations and personnel not specifically identified have been disguised.

British cities of Glastonbury and Avalon illustrate the world of hard business facts and the world of interrelated, sensitive humanity that should coexist in every enterprise. Both Glastonbury and Avalon also live in each of us. The quality of our daily experience and our power to define the future depend on our ability to deal with the factual world as it is and to form loyal, committed, and spiritually uplifting relationships.

The light cast by Merlin allows us to see, experience, and affirm Glastonbury and Avalon at the same time. It provides a way to simplify experience in an increasingly complex business environment. It also calls for us to take work out of the realm of the ordinary and make it a quest in which individuals' expression and material success join in strategic intent. Then—and even before then—Merlin vanishes: *Merlin's goal is to do himself out of a job.*

The Merlin process, developed over 25 years of research and experimentation into methods of defining the future, has proven effective on two continents. With roots in both Eastern and Western philosophy and folklore, Merlin has worked extensively and productively with North American and European businesses to improve their organizational and social systems. Besides the Arthurian legends, the Merlin process bases itself in many other systems, both ancient and modern. These include not only archetypal approaches such as those of Gestalt therapy,[2] Zen Buddhism, Yoga, meditation, and Native American cultures, but also the pragmatic contributions made by studies of decision making under uncertain conditions, dispute resolution, and controlled communication, as well as insights from computer science, existentialism, linguistics, and quantum physics.

The Merlin Factor discusses Arthur as a prototype for the modern man or woman who takes responsibility for an entire enterprise. The fact that the examples of corporate officials and leaders cited in *The Merlin Factor* are all male in no way means that a woman cannot serve as her organization's Arthur; it simply reflects the lamentable fact that none of the organizations with which this Merlin has interacted were led by women. And, according

---

[2]Particularly as analyzed by Erving and Miriam Polster (1973).

to a list comprising the 1,000 Fortune 500 companies and savings institutions, but two of the top 1,000 are headed by female chief executive officers, and only a few more than half of the Fortune 500 companies have a woman on their corporate boards (Catalyst, 1994). Women are considerably better represented at slightly lower levels of the corporate ranks, however, according to figures compiled by the National Foundation for Women Business Owners and Dun and Bradstreet Information Services (1995). In part, this study reports that "women-owned businesses now employ 35 percent more people in the United States than the Fortune 500 companies employ worldwide . . . [and] . . . now number 7.7 million. . . . [Women-owned businesses] provide jobs for 15.5 million people and generate nearly $1.4 trillion in sales . . ." (p. 2). For the time being, however, the masculine pronoun usually used here simply responds to the current reality that most chief executives—and *all* those with whom I have worked—have been men; I hope that the second edition of *The Merlin Factor* will reflect my own future experience working with chief executive officers and other leaders of both genders. *Nothing written here about Arthur applies only to half of humankind.*

Consistently transcending self-limiting beliefs, always open to mentoring by Merlin and his own knights, the corporate Arthur engages with concerns that most would avoid. Although he draws on the wisdom of legend and archetype, he faces everyday problems. There is nothing like a real issue (as opposed to a hypothetical one) to test judgment and identify priorities.

Some people, while intrigued by the prospect of adventure, draw back when they recognize what action could be necessary. Quickly realizing that their own inconstant purpose will be their undoing, they refuse the Arthurian imperative, with its commitment to build an ever-expanding Round Table aimed at previously unimaginable heights of achievement and spiritual satisfaction. In their quest for the Round Table, the knights are described as "living mirrors," who reflect Arthur's intentions and who, at their best, combine deep loyalty with their individual intentions and independence of mind. In a developed Round Table, Arthur and the knights project and mirror an organization that succeeds, sets an example, and has a heart. Those who take the path of excitement and discomfort choose to deal with the demons and dragons that oppose change in companies or themselves.

When Glastonbury and Avalon merge in the Round Table, the company finds itself in Camelot, which is not so much a place as a moment in time when life is a work of art. Camelot happens when great accomplishment, surprise, and cooperative effort brilliantly coalesce to acknowledge that "this is a great place to be." Michael Jordan, the heroic and graceful basketball star, spoke from Camelot when, in response to a question about how it felt to score 55 points while leading his team to victory, he said, "I am in my dreamland when I am playing. I love this game."

Camelot is everyone's dreamland. We have all been there; most, however, not often or long enough. Camelot is why I wrote *The Merlin Factor*. Business, the most powerful institution in the world, can—if it operates simultaneously from the measurable world of Glastonbury and the relational/spiritual world of Avalon—open the gates to Camelot.

If Camelot can flourish in corporate cultures, it can be realized anywhere.

1 ▪ THE MERLIN FACTOR

For, as I say, the world itself has changed. There was a time when a traveller, if he had the will and knew only a few of the secrets, could send his barge out into the Summer Sea and arrive not at the Glastonbury of the monks, but at the Holy Isle of Avalon; for at that time the gates between the worlds drifted within the mists, and were open, one to another, as the traveller thought and willed. For this was the great secret, which was known to all educated men in our day: that by what men think, we create the world around us, daily new. (Marion Zimmer Bradley, 1982, p.ix, quoting King Arthur's sister)

ndeed, the world has changed and must change again. Shortly after the time of King Arthur, most people forgot the great secret Morgan Le Fay describes of how to navigate between the visible and invisible dimensions of reality. The attempt to find that link, to forge a more meaningful whole of originally split parts, is a recurring theme in Western civiliza-

tion. Every social revolution—from the American and French rebellions to the movements for union and human rights—attempts to join spirit and body, to unite mind and soul, to balance material opportunity and personal liberty. Every time anyone jumps a personal or professional rut to "follow your bliss" (Joseph Campbell, 1988), he or she seeks that wholeness. Organizations trying to balance empowerment and order aim for a parallel link; upon it depends the health of people and organizations. The gates between the worlds must be opened again, and that lost secret is the key.

In Arthurian legend, Glastonbury symbolized a visible city and Avalon, an invisible city. Both, however, occupied the same physical territory. Only a few individuals like Merlin still knew how to find their way between the two. In fact, most people no longer even knew of Avalon's existence, let alone how to get there.

One of my theses is that, by analogy, each of today's corporations includes these same two dimensions. In a corporation's visible Glastonbury are found familiar objects and events, such as buildings, machines, raw materials, products, services, vendors, customers, and stock prices. Also there, unfortunately, often reside a host of problems. In the same company's invisible Avalon are relational qualities such as mutual trust, honesty, compassionate listening, forgiveness and reconciliation, caring relationships, cooperation toward grand visions, confidence in the future, alignment[3] among personnel, and commitment to others' success. Avalon, too, however, harbors difficulties. Both dimensions have their own cultures and structures, forms of energy, and outputs.

It is my belief that both Glastonbury and Avalon are essential to the vibrant health, genuine success, and continuous improvement of any organization. Glastonbury deals primarily with an organization's objective reality, with things tangible and countable. Avalon is most concerned with its relational realities, which are generally neither physical nor measurable.

---

[3]Among Webster's definitions of "alignment" is "arrangement in a straight line." While that may be the metaphorical end of corporate alignment, I am using the term here to describe shared commitment to a goal or goals.

Without Glastonbury, a corporation cannot offer products and services to its customers. Without Avalon, it will lack heart and soul.

Both individuals and organizations are systems that move naturally toward higher levels of complexity as they age. At any point in time, too much order, certainty, and prearranged process can suppress energy. So can too much flexibility, looseness, and emotion. Organizations and people need as much energy as possible to achieve their highest purposes. Typically, however, both respond to increased complexity by reflexively increasing—or trying to increase—order and process, *even when the problems are essentially relational, and they would be better off tending to their Avalons.* Some others try to deal with difficulties by becoming more flexible, adaptive, and open, *when their conflict might be best eased by a focus on the Glastonbury qualities of order and measuring.*

Usually, the reaction to complexity comes from a preexisting bias of the leadership, no matter what the cause of the problem. The Merlin Factor provides a simultaneous view of both sides. It refuses to be caught in one perspective and to consider it as the whole. Merlin can see what is missing in a company's Avalon and Glastonbury and guide others' energies toward strategic intent.

+═

UNITING TWO KINGDOMS

Recently, a multinational accounting firm sought a way to operate simultaneously from the consciousness of Avalon and Glastonbury. As an experiment, during a two-day workshop, its management team deliberately raised their consciousness about each dimension alternately. The team spent two hours on cash flow problems, two hours in self-development exercises, two hours in strategic planning, two hours in expressing appreciation of one another, two hours on a current legal entanglement, two hours on poetry, two hours on technical design, and so on.

Rather than finding they had wasted half their time on nonproductive relational activity, participants said the session was the most effective business meeting they had ever had. Never had their confidence in meeting the next year's sales and profit goals been higher; never was their shared trust that each would do his/her part firmer.

As the session proceeded, the group's vision of their company as a single, undivided reality increased dramatically. Their world view had changed. By the end of the meeting, Glastonbury and Avalon had ceased to exist as limitations to each other's domains. People who had complained about the lack of focus and orderly process were delighted; so were those who had missed team spirit and leadership.

Raising consciousness of Avalon and Glastonbury successively and sometimes simultaneously had at first been confusing. As the new category of thought became clearer, however, the group's experience changed. Individuals became able to operate from a place that included Glastonbury and Avalon but was neither. The whole, Camelot, was greater than its parts. This firm had discovered the Merlin Factor.

The problem is that most people don't see Avalon and Glastonbury at the same time. We tend to think in either/or terms, especially under pressure. Merlin's power comes from the ability simultaneously to hold these opposites in mind with equal force. This task, which takes commitment and practice, is as much about money as it is about relationships and as much about process as about culture. In Camelot, accountability for results is as important as generous listening (see pages 128–133). Learning is as essential as accomplishment; discovering one's own past, as vital as fulfilling a collective intent.

In the business-as-usual universe, people *either* speak the truth from their heart, *or* they talk business. They *either* build teams, *or* they interact individually. None of these opposites works by itself, and the lopsided practitioner usually ends up paying a price either in efficiency and effectiveness or through conflict and emotional abuse.

If leaders operate solely from Glastonbury, they treat people as things, and the price in human energy, creativity, and misalignment can be enormous. If leaders operate only from Avalon, they handle both people and things too gently, while measurement, productivity, focus, coordination, and results often suffer.

Trust in Glastonbury demands performance and results; trust in Avalon requires emotional support. Both are needed in a vibrant and successful enterprise. It is difficult to hold on to the paradoxical reality of Camelot that insists on tending to results and caring at the same time. When leaders' minds come to be simultaneously open to both realities, they can serve at once as stewards to their organizations' Avalons and guardians of their Glastonburys. Then occurs a fundamental shift in the quality of a corporation's life and effectiveness. If corporate Camelot became the norm, its spirit could soon extend to families, communities, governments, and international relations.

The world needs a quantum shift in the way people think. This change should be sudden; we need not wait for gradual mutation or for dramatic social or economic crises to bring it about. It is especially critical in the leaders who control societies' most valued resources and whose personal orientation to Avalon and Glastonbury affects the lives and productivity of millions of people.

⊷⊶

GLASTONBURY

In this book, Glastonbury is an organizational metaphor for integrity. Organizations without a bottom line seem to be less efficient and effective in their operations than those that have an unequivocal way of measuring their success. Without the integrity of measured outcomes, emotion tends to hold sway over intellect, and the expression of deeply held values can replace a commitment to results. Because every organization is a physical entity, however, it must be located in time and space. Measurement assures existence, and Glastonbury reflects the integrity that can only exist when something is measured. People are on time or they are not, make money or don't, work in a clean place or don't.

Almost everyone has a personal relationship, encountered early and shaped by personal experience, with both Avalon and Glastonbury.

Glastonbury at Its Best

The optimum Glastonbury is an honorable place where all detail matters. Careful attention to physical detail releases people's physical, emotional, mental, and spiritual energies into great richness and variety. James W. Rouse, founder in the late 1930s of the Rouse Company (one of the nation's largest publicly held real estate development and management companies) wears a number of hats. Retired as chairman of the Rouse board in 1979, he currently works as founder-chairman of the Enterprise Foundation, which devotes itself to creating low-cost housing. His statement captures Glastonbury's essential contribution:

> I am committed that the lives of people and communities for generations to come will be affected by what we do; that the surest road to success is to discover the authentic needs and yearnings of people and do our best to service them; that people seek warm and human places with diversity and charm, full of festival and delight; that they are degraded by tacky, tasteless places and are oppressed by coldness and indifference; that they are uplifted by the creative caring which that demands; that we believe everything matters; that all detail is important.(personal communication, 1995)

In this spirit, among the Rouse Company's rich achievements are many malls and urban market places (including Boston's Faneuil Hall and Baltimore's Harborplace) and the very successful satellite city of Columbia, Maryland, where the company is located.

And in the Rouse spirit is the fascinating Disney World in Orlando, Florida. I have visited there at least 15 times—alone, with my children, and with clients. According to research ("Lessons from Mickey Mouse," 1994; Neil Baum, 1992), I am not alone in my frequent revisits. About 75 percent of those who visit Disney are returnees. To maintain this high return rate, the parks must regularly meet and frequently exceed customer expectations.

For years, my consulting company was able to do impressive initial work with clients, helping them create great dreams, visions, partnerships, and images of the future. We enlisted the entire organization and implemented values through strategic projects that germinated culture change. Then, frequently, something failed to happen. Too often, the company's follow-through was weak, and its assimilation of the values to which it had so eagerly committed in the beginning, incomplete. Inertia seemed to take over.

This didn't happen at the Disney theme parks. What was different? To answer that question, I began to study Disney World and came up with two new questions:

- How did Disney personnel build such a desirable Glastonbury culture that its vitality lasted, while others diminished?
- How did they create such a brilliant material container for their vision and values?

Answers began to emerge. Disney's success appeared to originate in executives and employees' willingness to assimilate company values and maintain their momentum through positive behavior. The expectation that Disney staff embrace Disney values is made clear in application interviews, first-day orientations, extensive training courses, measurement of work, and the complex feedback forms provided to each employee ("Disney's Recruitment," 1992).

On one occasion, I stepped aboard an empty Disney bus and noticed a piece of scrap paper on the floor. I automatically picked it up and gave it to the bus driver, who put it in a waste bin. Realizing, as we rode along, that my gesture was curious and uncommon, I recalled that, the day before, I had overheard a smiling, pretty young woman explain, "Everybody helps keep Disney World clean. The guests keep it clean; the employees keep it clean. The average time a piece of trash remains on the ground in Disney World is 18 seconds." I was mentally living in a clean place, and I found myself spontaneously—and proudly—helping to keep it like that.

Why?

The atmosphere seemed to derive from Walt Disney's devotion to "putting on a good show." The staff at Disney World asked each other frequently whether particular acts or objects made up a good show or not.

Either they did, or they didn't. A good show is going out of one's way to help someone, keeping one's office or other work space orderly, picking up stray papers. A bad show is acting discourteously, forgetting to put up a caution sign when mopping the floor, dropping a gum wrapper. Disney World's "good show," a way of talking about quality performance, has the advantage of being deeply embedded in ordinary vocabulary. The "good show" is achieved through staff commitment to certain explicit service standards—*safety, efficiency, courtesy, show* ("Disney's Recruitment," 1992). These standards are core values expressed in easily observable actions.

That these standards—particularly courtesy—also hail from Avalon is a core reason for Disney World's success. But its fundamental values come from Glastonbury; they are part of an expert drama. There is nothing the matter with this: Is *Romeo and Juliet* invalid because the actor and actress on stage are not really in love (or, for that matter, really dead, at the drama's end)? Did Fred Astaire and Ginger Rogers dance less gloriously because they didn't spend their free time together? Disney World's Glastonbury is its "good show," a universe that at its peak of excellence integrates Avalon's energies into its enabling physical container.

That Disney emphasizes measurability and visible performance (Glastonbury qualities) does not preclude Avalon's existence there; the park teaches us a profound truth about the power of positive human experience—planned or spontaneous. For example, when customers feel safe everywhere in the park, they might risk taking an amusement ride that looks scary. If everything there runs *efficiently*, customers will expect to enjoy themselves without any trouble, confusion, or unnecessary delay. Customers treated *courteously* feel valued and are likely to want to come back, to recommend the park, and to bring others with them. A *good show* will likely make ambassadors of Disney's customers.

In a sense, Disney World has Glastonburied Avalon!

People working at Disney, whether part- or full-time, long- or short-service, *seem* happy and pleased to be there. I can't honestly tell if they are *really* happy or whether their smiles are part of the entertainment. From the customer's point of view, however, that doesn't usually matter. And, although wages at Disney World are not high, workers seem to like being on stage and in the entertainment business so much that their low salaries become unimportant. They seem proud to work at a place so obviously a stunning success.

Walt Disney once said, "Find out what the people want and build it for them," and he meant it. Surprisingly, this attitude is rare in the business world. In spite of rhetoric about the customer coming first, most companies operate out of their own frameworks. It's what the executives, or Wall Street, or the regulators, or the stockholders—not what the customers—want that is the beacon guiding operations. As one executive admitted to me, "We can't even listen to the customer when we have other things on our mind."

Maintaining momentum toward greatness is a crucial factor in Glastonbury. Disney is able to achieve excellent follow-through because it has institutionalized its service standards. The park's rewards, training, and language cement the standards' pervasiveness though orientation, acknowledgment, and leadership. These four service standards are not upheld *some* of the time, or even *most* of the time, but *all* of the time. This level of attention to physical detail is one of Glastonbury's greatest strengths.

Every company aspires to Glastonbury virtues, but, while many try to be specific, measurable, appealing, relevant, and prompt, not every one succeeds. The matter seems fundamentally simple: After all, why not just be specific? Why not just come on time? The problem is that Glastonbury at its best is a *context*, not merely a matter of improving process, structure, and procedures. Context is another word for fundamental commitments.

SEEING BEYOND GLASTONBURY TO AVALON

As Glastonbury stands for the integrity of things measurable in a corporation, so Avalon stands for the integrity of things nonmeasurable: harmony, cooperation, commitment, joy, presence, authority, congruence, freedom, truth, healing, trust, and so on. In Glastonbury, phenomena are located in measurable time and space. People use clocks to measure time and streets to define location, but one cannot place "caring" in chronological time or linear space: Care exists—or it does not—*between* individuals. In Avalon, phenomena exist in the realm of between, a different dimension, a separate state of consciousness. Like gravity, relationships can't be seen directly, but their effect shows they're there.

Trying to draw a unified purpose from a divided kingdom was Arthur's main task. It is also that of most corporate leaders. This task is accomplished simultaneously in two worlds or dimensions. For a corporation to undergo a quality transformation, leadership has to commit to altering its processes fundamentally and to improving its customer focus continually in visible Glastonbury. At the same time, people in the corporation must shift to relate to each other at the level of heart and spirit in unseen Avalon.

⊶

AVALON

Avalon is the world of attraction and repulsion among individuals in an organization relating to one another. I sometimes feel at odds with corporate leaders and managers who act as if the only reality is the one they see—paychecks, tools, authorities, buildings, schedules, reports, and so forth. Avalon's vital universe remains unseen to many.

To create a Round Table, a corporate kingdom, chivalry among knights, greatness, something memorable, leaders must develop this invisible but crucially important dimension of the corporation. Avalon is the intricate complex of relationships among all the persons in the organization. Each individual has a relationship to self, to the past, to the future, to a family of origin and/or by marriage, to fellow employees and teams at work, to the company as a whole, and to the work itself. In addition to these relationships, individuals also make commitments to values that promote relationships, such as trust, love, quality, honesty, and patience. (Values that can confound close relationships include freedom, self-reliance, control, privacy, and equity.) All such value choices have an impact on relationships, either enabling them or setting boundaries.

A relationship isn't real when it is being observed or analyzed; it exists and operates only when people share it. The minute someone tries, scientifically, to examine a relationship, s/he has stepped out of it, out of Avalon, into Glastonbury. Observing a relationship changes it, in the same way that a writer must become a critic to evaluate his or her story, essay, or poem.

Avalon at Its Best

Tony Turnbull, for a number of years plant manager of a European branch of Procter and Gamble, integrated Avalon's dimensions into his career. Turnbull proved to be the best corporate champion for culture change I have ever met.

Two years after taking over the plant, he was given orders to close down a nearby sister installation that employed 170 people, including first- and second-level managers, clerical and technical staff, and plant technicians. There were only six vacancies at his plant. This was the first time the company had ever declared lay-offs.

The closing Turnbull oversaw was unique in that it was accomplished not only with full Glastonbury accountability, but also with abundant consciousness of Avalon's priorities. The process made possible the ultimate success of the company's efforts to meet its responsibility for assisting the departing staff and to preserve their good relationship with the company. While people were leaving the company, all-time production records were set. Still, operations terminated at—or before—the preagreed times. Everyone had learned at the outset that the plant's closing would be in line with effective business practices and deadlines. There would be no softening or compromise in customer service, quality, operational safety, or production goals; this approach promoted empowerment as well as sound business values. Remembered Turnbull,

> First of all, I realized that I needed to "choose" to do this closure in its totality as though it had been my own decision and not something I had been asked to do by a higher authority.
> I worked at ensuring that I had total understanding and"ownership" of

the decision, including not only being able to explain how the decision was in line with the corporate and business strategies at the European, not just the UK, level, but also why it was the right thing to do for the future of the company. I wanted to promulgate this rationale, not as though I or the company claimed divine foresight, but rather as the very best plan we could see for the future of the company as a whole.

I consulted with my boss and his boss and anyone else I considered necessary, until I was personally satisfied that the proper research, thinking, consideration, and preparation had preceded the conclusion to close the plant.

Once I was satisfied, I proceeded to work with each of my managers who would be involved in the closure process, both in groups and individually, asking them to adopt the same mentality if they could. I promised the individual managers that they would not be asked to manage the shutdown, unless they fully chose it as though it were their own decision.

I didn't take their "yes" reply at face value. In the end, one admitted that he couldn't fully choose the closing, and I accepted that without making him feel wrong. All the managers understood that by saying "yes" and meaning "no" they would indeed let me down and, more importantly, let the team down when the going got tough.

Then, over a period of three months, the managers and I spent several days off-site working through what we planned to do and say. We rigorously tested the steps of our plan against company principles and core values as well as against our own principles and values. Whenever we found inconsistency, we struggled with the problem until we changed our plan or were able, authentically, to say we were acting in line with our principles.

These sessions proved to be very difficult and often went on late into the night, but I believe they provided the bedrock for everything we did afterwards. Managers were no longer acting under instructions from me but out of what they believed was the right thing to do.

Among Turnbull's other approaches from Avalon:

… The conditions under which we helped those let go find new jobs required them to cooperate with us. This meant, for example, they had to go to all of the job interviews we arranged, take new training if necessary, be flexible in running the plant during this period, and so on.

⤳ We got creative about finding jobs for people and did some unthinkable things. Though we sometimes broke company rules and policies, we never violated company principles. In instances when we bent the rules, we tried to get corporate agreement first, but in some cases I authorized apparent irregularities without approval from headquarters.

⤳ The employees themselves got into the spirit of the game and came up with all sorts of ideas. One of the best was that I should go to company headquarters and personally ask everyone, from the president down to the clerks, to give meat least one powerful reference for a job opening. Headquarters came up with 50 references, and about 10 of these resulted in jobs.

⤳ We convinced the local job center to give us the list of new job openings two hours before it went public, and we taxied our people down there immediately. This worked for about three months, until some higher-up in the local government found out and stopped it. But by then we had already placed several people.

⤳ We talked other companies into taking some of our people on a one- or two-week trial basis with the agreement that we would take them back if it didn't work out. Only one ever came back.

⤳ We arranged for other companies to come into our plant to interview people.

⤳ We arranged paid visits for employees and their families to apply for vacancies at distant company locations as far as 200–300 miles away. We arranged for the local housing authorities and schools there to provide tours of the area. Only three or four vacancies were filled this way, but the impact on the employees' families was immeasurable in building respect for and trust in the company. It also gave the employees' spouses an opportunity to say directly to me and other mangers how they felt about the whole thing.

⤳ We took every employee through an analysis of his or her financial situation before and after the closing. Most people are in such a state of shock when they know they're going to be let go that they can't do a rational financial analysis. Some think they are going to be wiped out forever, while others look forward to spending their entire severance pay quickly and with great abandon.

- ❧ I met with every single person affected, personally and continually, to ensure that I was totally present to the process, without taking away any manager's authority. I apologized to employees for any broken promises the company or I may have made to them. I was also able to clarify whether promises had, in fact, been broken, or whether the employees' interpretation was faulty.

- ❧ To help me complete the process in the most compassionate way possible, I visited other companies to learn what they had done in similar situations. I found a manager in Belfast, Northern Ireland, who, while conducting a shut down operation, had found a job for every one of his 500 people. These visits inspired me and helped me to keep thinking creatively, even if I didn't copy exactly what they had done.

- ❧ I asked my managers to treat each person in the way they would wish to be treated. I promised them the same consideration if their time came.

- ❧ I insisted that we manage the process ourselves. Even though we did use consultants and advisors to help us, they were never allowed to take over management.

I was one of those consultants Turnbull mentions. The fact that I didn't have to visit the plant very frequently was a sign that they were doing well by themselves. By the time they were ready to implement the processes they had worked out, they didn't really need me. As I wrote earlier, Merlin's goal is to do himself out of a job (see page 2).

Here are some of the promises coming from Avalon in the service of Glastonbury that Turnbull and his managers made to themselves about the effect they hoped the shutdown would have on the people being let go.

- ❧ If we met any of these people on the street two years after they had left, they would shake our hands and speak with pride about having been a company employee. They would acknowledge the respect and dignity with which we treated their leaving, and they would still encourage their children and others to join the company.

- ❧ The people who were transferred to the new plant would feel reassured about how they would be treated should a similar downsizing happen to them there. It did, and they were!

- We would treat everyone fairly, though this did not mean they would all be treated in exactly the same way. Each person would be treated as an individual with particular needs and concerns. Thus, some departing employees received the specialized training necessary to help them find new jobs; others, wanting to start up their own businesses, received equipment or materials (such as computers and old packaging equipment) from us to facilitate that process.
- Everyone would receive a similar financial package. Though the amounts would differ, the severance pay would rank among the best in the local area.
- The method of selection would be clear to everyone and would be designed according to what was best for the company's future. Given our commitment to a win-win outcome, we rarely found it necessary to compromise in favor of the company's future. I can recall only 2 such cases out of 170.
- Nobody would be put out on the street without a job who did not say s/he wanted to retire.

In the end, Turnbull and his management team received many positive comments from the people affected by the shutdown. He particularly remembers

a 45-year-old man with many years of service who came to me the day he was leaving to thank me for the way we had handled the whole process. He said that he wanted me to know that in 25 years he had never realized the commitment his manager had to him until he experienced his help and support during this time.

I tell this story in great detail because it shows so well the creative energy that can come from a commitment to Avalon values. This wary group of managers, faced with a sad and daunting task, actually enhanced and strengthened relationships between employees—past and present—and the company. "It's not that I would want to have to do this again," Turnbull admitted, "but if it were needed, I would do it the same way, but even more so."

Turnbull's story differs markedly from many other "downsizings." Often, people are not informed of their job loss until the day of their departure. Personal apology is rarely forthcoming from the company, and the job of healing and follow-up is left to out-placement consultants. When such an exercise is designed from Glastonbury's cost and effectiveness considerations in the absence of Avalon's commitments, regardless of the benefits package and rhetoric, many people end up feeling like used objects being discarded.

Turnbull's management team were champions of Avalon.

King Arthur confronts the material and physical circumstances of a situation as well as the relational ones. Turnbull and his management team not only talked compassionately to the people but also went to bat for them, helping them find jobs. If the financial circumstances of a situation are demoralizing, Arthur strives to fix the material situation, while still generously listening and speaking truth from the heart.

Among Turnbull and his company's intentions was to treat the situation so that even the long-term effect of the shutdown would be positive. To do so, they looked for each person's truth, especially the truth the employee could not see for him- or herself at the time. Arthur, committed to Avalon, dedicates himself to the truth of the situation. Turnbull and his team did some remarkable listening, with each other and with the individual employees affected. They kept operating from a positive future for each person and accepted responsibility for the success of the relationship between employees and the company.

If excellence in Glastonbury is rooted in "profound knowledge" (W. Edwards Deming's phrase, see page 33), excellence in Avalon is based in profound relationship, a reality every bit as real, as influential, and with as much potential for good or evil as Glastonbury's. Avalon as a context is quite equal to Glastonbury. The nature of the field of play defines the game. A tennis court or a football field tells the viewer which sport is to be played there. It is not enough to *talk* about Avalon: Those who wish to influence corporate cultures must clarify Avalon's sphere in the corporation so that people notice and experience it.

I once saw a cartoon that showed two doorways. The first doorway, marked "Heaven," had almost no one in front of it. The second doorway, marked "Lecture on Heaven," had a long line of people waiting to get inside. Most people would prefer to hear about paradise than face the personal challenges and self-development it would take to actually experience it.

Similarly, most are willing to talk about Avalon, but few are eager to go there. It takes a great deal of effort and dedication to enter the gateways to Avalon and play by its rules. In the beginning, however, it is enough that people are willing to have a conversation about Avalon; at least they are open to believing that it exists.

You Can't Go There Alone

Avalon consists of all the genuine relationships within a company as well as relationships with those closely related to it, such as suppliers, distributors, customers, and so forth. Avalon often appears evanescent, because it does not seem to persist. But unless you are creating or fostering relationships, Avalon doesn't happen. It fades into the mists. As soon as the champions of Avalon disappear, so does Avalon. Turnbull's team really wanted to create Avalon, and they were willing to work hard to keep it in existence. In so doing, however, they in no way ignored the priorities of Glastonbury.

Avalon's Energies

Just as Glastonbury has its unique energies, reflected in commitments to safety, efficiency, courtesy, good show, beauty, order, and detail, so Avalon has its unique kinds of energies, such as honesty, trust, connectedness, harmony through conflict, truth telling, shared intention, healing, reconciliation, and alignment.

Avalon's energies are all relational, connecting people to each other heart to heart. Certain Glastonbury energies are often mistakenly viewed as expressions of Avalon. These include smiles, handshakes, hearty greetings, polite conversation, holding doors open for people, offering coffee or other refreshment, pointing out safety precautions, being on time, showing patience, agreeing, and so on.

Each of these actions is clearly an expression of the Glastonbury energies of courtesy, safety, cleanliness, good show, and attention to detail. So are going together to a ball game, playing golf, and having lunch. None, however, requires commitment to a relationship nor to the success of the other person. None requires that anyone speak the truth from the heart or listen with genuine compassion. None requires cocreation of a future. None requires that anyone align with others as committed colleagues toward a shared purpose.

In Avalon, the substance of relationship is not agreement but *alignment*. Agreement is a simple mental action; alignment implies unity. Attainment of a shared goal, purpose, or strategic intent is the basis for alignment. Only that shared aim is worth the interpersonal effort it takes to align. The substance of relationship in Glastonbury is *agreement*, that is, the willingness of people to modify their minds and beliefs so that all the people involved can reach consensus. Agreement, by no means a dishonorable goal, is not the substance of Avalon.

THE DARK SIDES

Negative energies occur in Avalon as well, but their shadows differ dramatically from those typical of Glastonbury. For example, those who live only in Glastonbury can find themselves enmeshed in internal competition, thinking in terms of hierarchies or scarcity, looking for and finding scapegoats. In contrast, those stuck only in Avalon have little concern for product and result, set unrealistic goals, avoid danger, will not inquire, lack ambition, and respond with passive aggression toward people asking that they perform.

Many people think that the world of Glastonbury is the only real one, and, superficially, this can look true. Things can be touched, seen, heard, felt, and counted in Glastonbury, while affirming the palpable reality of invisible Avalon contradicts sense perceptions. Glastonbury stands in sunlight; Avalon is hidden in mist.

In many corporations, Avalon resides uneasily within the prevailing Glastonbury. Those in a company focused on performance and money often have little patience with those committed to listening and dialogue. Citizens carrying sole or primary Glastonbury loyalties might characterize ideas from Avalon residents as "too soft," "touchy-feely," or "irrelevant." Further, Glastonbury might complain of Avalon,

- "Those people pay too little attention to results."
- "Their countless hours in flavor-of-the-month training programs and workshops are one of the reasons our company is in so much trouble."
- "This too will make no difference."
- "Let's go back to work, where the real stuff happens."

Many a corporate Glastonbury accords no honor to corporate Avalon. Instead, Avalon suffers disrespect, complaint, suppression, and/or outright hostility. In the same way, those stuck in Avalon for their part have little compassion for their companions in Glastonbury. Like nagging spouses, they are antagonistic and self-righteous. In cases like these, as in a stressful marriage, Avalon feels misunderstood and suppressed, and Glastonbury feels judged and criticized.

One aspect of the solution is to encourage those whose loyalties are tilted toward Avalon to respect the world of production and technology: Avalon often accuses Glastonbury of treating people like objects or functionaries. Without understanding its contributions, winning Glastonbury's heart as well as mind is impossible, and there is little other hope for the corporation that needs an alignment its eyes cannot see.

The solution also requires compromise from those with primary loyalties to Glastonbury. They must come to honor the relational world of Avalon where people are treated as persons—indeed, as sacred beings. Only when they are thus treated do men and women truly want to unite their energies, in a corporation or anywhere else.

⊬

Two Spheres

Historical Glastonbury, which dated from Roman times, was where—according to legend—Joseph of Arimathea, who was also thought to have brought the Holy Grail to Britain, was said to have established the first Christian Church in England. When Joseph planted his staff, it took root, becoming the Glastonbury thorn that blossoms every Christmas Eve. The historical Arthur is thought to be buried in the ruins of Glastonbury Cathedral, where he was taken after his final battle with Mordred. Arthur's spirit is said to reside on the holy island of Avalon, from which he is expected to return.

Normal talk in corporate Glastonbury includes debate, lecture, explanation, analysis, opinion, assessment, accountability, business process, strategy, polite conversation, technological talk, and so on. Normal talk in Avalon includes dialogue, speculation, commitment, inquiry, coinvention, sharing, intention, inspiration, forgiveness, reconciliation, and so on. In Glastonbury, although ideally people are treated politely and with respect, they are seen primarily as objects, instruments, or functionaries—parts of the corporate engine—in the service of the system. Avalon sees each person as "Thou," in the sense Martin Buber used the pronoun, as someone deserving total attention and unconditional regard (1923/1978; 1947/1985).

Glastonbury operates in *kronos*, that is, in linear or clock time; this is evident in its dedication to planning. Avalon operates in *kairos*, that is, sacred time, the timeless moment. In Avalon, one can step into the future, speak and listen, and act; then step back from the reality of that future without feeling trapped by present circumstances or history. Merlin, portrayed in T. H. White's *The Once and Future King*, and Stanley M. Davis's *Future Perfect* [1990], explains how he can paradoxically "remember the future." (See also page 124.)

This timelessness, paradoxically, is a finite, identifiable Avalon event in time and space. It occurs when a group or pair of people enter, together, a shared state of consciousness that might, for example, be manifest in moments of coinvention, in sharing profound personal truths, in generous listening, in speculation or celebration of shared accomplishment. During such an Avalon event, people experience a collective, relational oneness of mind and heart that no individual can feel alone. Such an event might occur during a meeting whose participants' thoughts and feelings are aligned.

+≔

THE BEST OF BOTH WORLDS

Two fundamental points of view about where to start to change an organization appear contradictory on the surface but they are both valid. The first, from Glastonbury, says that instituting effective processes will produce the desired changes. According to this logic, problems with relationships in the organization are best dealt with as a concomitant of process. The second, from Avalon, says that changing relationships will more rapidly produce the desired results. According to this logic, process problems are best dealt with as a concomitant of relationships. Defending either point of view as the right one is fruitless, polarizes opposing advocates, and limits access to the truths offered by the other view.

Process reengineering happens in Glastonbury. Culture change happens in Avalon. Revitalizing an organization requires both. Without effective process, the organizational train is without a track. Without committed, open relationships, the track will be strewn with rocks, other debris, even occasional land mines, and the change effort will be repeatedly derailed.

+≔

THE ROUND TABLE

A Round Table can be created only from Avalon, when Arthur and an ever-expanding circle of knights unite across an organization in a desirable new cultural pattern. They acknowledge that their commitment to the quality of relationship in the organization (Avalon) is as important to them as quality process and company profits, products, and services (Glastonbury).

The Round Table includes both. Understanding the function of both cultures in a company is essential to forging an aligned organization. Forgetting the importance of Avalon often leads to failure in strategic planning efforts, even when all the right players are present.

A corporate culture is the set of beliefs, attitudes, values, procedures, and practices that people consistently reinforce in thought, word, and action as true, right, appropriate, and important. It binds them together as an identifiable and enduring group and shapes their behavior, reactions, responses, expectations, disappointments, trust and mistrust, closeness and distance, freedom and fear. It creates the options from within which people choose and plan.

In a company's everyday reality, the Glastonbury culture is always operating. It affects the thinking, behavior, responses, choices and plans people make. It colors the way each person does his or her job and how they relate to other individuals, teams and departments within the organization. A Glastonbury culture may be unique to the organization, or it may reflect the larger culture common to the local community, state, or nation. If the latter, it is often characterized by mistrust, fear, competition, control, and resentment.

Even senior officials often fail to understand the essential and interrelated power of a company's Glastonbury and Avalon cultures. Both are always present but, because the Avalon culture is not material, it is not "real" to many people. Few can spell out their actual current corporate rules and assumptions in their Glastonbury and Avalon cultures with any degree of completeness. They are like fish in a lake whose culture is the water in which they swim. Fish take the water so much for granted that only when one is pulled out does it realize it has lost, or changed, its culture, *or, indeed, even what it really means to be a fish.* People in companies similarly are often unable to recognize the culture they're in until they are at least partly removed from it.

It is very difficult to move out of a familiar culture to a new one. If the grip of history is too powerful, the cultural change process may fail, and, in the face of the best intentions, the force of the past ends up shaping the future. In other words, people stay in the same culture and context as they began. Just as fish will drown in a culture too foreign—air—corporate change too drastic can be fatal to the aims of the Round Table. To switch metaphors, members of a professional football team can reasonably be told that next season they will improve their performance, but they cannot expect that next April they will become a lacrosse team. And they can't play football on a baseball diamond.

In order to operate in a new context, Arthur and the knights must define its existence and work as if it is already functioning. As Gandhi and Martin Luther King, Jr., knew, peace must be created from a nonviolent base. Only members of a peaceful organization can create and maintain a harmonious future. One counsellor puts the rule this way: "Change the behavior and the reality follows." Rather like a shadow government that makes its own decisions, it is the organization of the future that reshapes current realities. To align the organization into a Round Table, Arthur and the knights—sometimes with Merlin's help—speak and listen from the future while continuing to operate effectively in the present.

Tomorrow cannot be predicted, but at any time it can be *defined*, as long as one's point of view is rooted in the desired future rather than the unwanted past. The person who frames the future rather than accepting someone else's vision becomes a champion rather than a victim.

J. A. ("Tony") Gilroy, now chief operating officer of the Varity Corporation, was managing director of a wildly successful Range Rover rebirth into the world market. His conviction that this vehicle would be the jewel in the crown of the British auto industry transformed the company and successfully introduced it into the United States.

Gilroy realized that yesterday's methods would not work, because

> We needed to change the internal and external perception of Land Rover. We needed a dealer network around the world to invest in completely altering our approach to servicing customers. Unless that happened, no matter what we did with the product, we wouldn't sell it. The results were unheard of. The volume doubled, and the price increased, with the introduction of the Range Rover into North America. This put

us into a different sector and increased our customers' satisfaction enormously.

This leadership experience led Gilroy to an executive position within the Perkins group of companies,[4] the world's third-largest diesel manufacturer, whose business success through quality implementation has also dramatically improved labor relations.

+—

ESSENTIAL AVALON

To paraphrase comedienne Lily Tomlin, no matter how cynical I get about a particular company culture, it's never cynical enough. Companies without Avalon's consciousness, no matter how good Glastonbury looks or how much money they make, cannot listen to others sensitively or leave them empowered. Ultimately, Glastonbury organizations find they have no platform on which their future can rest. Mikhail Gorbachev blamed his failure to be able to continue to lead the former USSR on his lack of sufficient attention to enlisting people's personal support (Thorsell, 1993).

Similarly, people without Glastonbury consciousness either live without a lot of money or are always in debt. I once worked as a fundraiser and management consultant in a Glastonbury-free organization, whose superb cause was eventually diluted through a combination of outside political opposition and internal inattention to good business process. Members of the staff, who earned little or no money in- or outside the organization, were compassionate, inefficient, and—often—personally in debt. Even its popular mission could not save this underfunded operation: The institutional train had no track on which to run.

The organization's poverty symbolized its disdain for Glastonbury. Staff members, who were far more committed to the cause than to funding the organization, failed to fulfill their intended mission. To succeed, the lead-

---

[4]On Perkins, see also page 128–129

ership would have to have been as cognizant of the company's physical and financial realities as committed to its ethical purposes. Their quest, based firmly in Avalon, was noble. It floundered for lack of Glastonbury virtues, however, serving no one.

SHIFTING STRUCTURES

Thomas S. Kuhn's analysis of the resistance with which new scientific paradigms often meet applies to the business world as well (1969). An organization's culture serves to preserve its already existing identity, and many of its members fear that changing it will ruin them. They usually have considerable evidence that the status quo is the reason why they have so far succeeded. General Motors, for example, held tenaciously to its fundamental commitment to large automobiles, well after all facts and figures indicated most Americans' dramatic shift toward preferring smaller cars and more efficient fuel consumption. IBM's slow shift from mainframes to compact personal computers is another example of inappropriate resistance to change.

Culture change introduces new myths.

To be effective, a culture change alters people's ways of relating to one another—how they view, listen to, talk to, behave toward one another—both within the organization and within interactions with customers and suppliers. It changes interaction in formal and informal situations, and it encourages mutual support and commitments. *Culture change originates only in Avalon.* It must have an impact both on the complex network of relationships in place and on the organization's collective memory of past relationships.

Cultural shifts are expressed and experienced, first of all, in relationships, in that curious *between* reality that ultimately shapes whether or not the company wins in the market, whether customers are satisfied, and whether employees are happy to be at work. Culture change is concretely experienced as heightened team spirit; it must be sustained or it disappears.

The grip of a corporate culture on individuals and teams is identical to the existing and remembered relationships within that corporation. For a culture to change, therefore, people's relationships have to change. This shift is so difficult to achieve that most culture-change efforts fail. Too few people can see new pathways to take, even if they are brave and industrious enough to interrelate differently.

Neither process reengineering nor structural reorganization will, by themselves, change people's experience of relationships. While a procedural solution to a procedural problem may work, a procedural solution to a relationship problem has little effect, except to further cynicism and resignation.

"Only Connect"[5]

The culture change begins with Arthur's and each of the knights' commitment to the success of their relationships throughout the company. Commitment here is an either/or situation: In any moment for any relationship, one is either committed to its success, or one is not. The relationship may be between two people, between an individual and a team, or between a person and everyone in the company.

The shallow, superficial professional relationships people in most companies tolerate compare unfavorably to those of Arthur and Merlin, of soldiers in combat, or even of good friends. They may privately feel more deeply than they demonstrate publicly, but their hidden emotions have little impact and can even fuel cynicism and resentment of perceived corporate repressiveness. "Protocols" and "appropriate organizational behavior" are generally defined as distant, not intimate, in today's atmosphere of legal restrictions and attention to interpersonal violation.

Deep relationships need not be warm, fuzzy ones, however. They can be based on mutual commitments; the need for coordinated activity or successful sales; the wish for companionship, a team, or a partnership; or concern

---

[5]E. M. Forster's advice, from Howard's End (1910/1981).

for someone or something else. Good relationships have countless bases.

As a result of the managers' commitment, the quality of the employees' experience during the shutdown of Turnbull's manufacturing plant was extraordinary. In contrast, most companies have too many employees acting like victims being persecuted or thanking God it's Friday.

To be a leader for culture change is to be committed to changing the nature of relationships in one's company. But few corporate leaders know how to get to Avalon themselves or how to lead others there. That's where Merlin comes in.

When I first meet with business leaders, I usually discover that most of them are not experiencing the relationships they want. From the point of view of corporate results, so long as the company is doing well financially, the lack of satisfying relationships is rarely seen as a problem. Moreover, since the present state of relationships (no matter how poor it may be) appears to be achieving current success, the idea of changing the ways people relate seems risky and threatening. "If it ain't broke, don't fix it," as the saying goes. But *is* it broke or not?

Beginning the process of culture change requires courage and the willingness to be vulnerable. But it is also often essential. As world markets globalize, populations grow, and technology complexifies, businesses are increasingly forced to change contexts and the ways they operate. Those wise enough to recognize that to change the quality of a corporate culture it is necessary to change the quality of its relationships can open the path to the magical kingdom of Avalon. Some can take on the role of Arthur on their own. Many need the help of Merlin.

From corporate Avalon, a kingdom can be unified and aligned; to the Round Table, people can give their hearts as well as their minds in a shared aim. One successful chief executive officer asks his employees to provide narratives of their professional and personal successes. He explains,

> In my company, we've created our own mythical city with its own magical behavior and expanding Round Table. We acknowledge the extraor-

dinary performance of our people through their stories. We solicit, then read and appreciate the stories that tell the extraordinary accomplishments of these people.

Their submissions, inspired by an Avalon concept, record hard, tangible (Glastonbury) results. And, says the executive, the rise in productivity is dramatic: People who said, "It's impossible," move to "It was easy." They have to take an incredible visionary leap, examining behavior recognized as perfectly fine in the past and deciding "It's no longer acceptable." After they tell me that there has to be a new and different way, they go and find the path *themselves*. For example, people who have complained to me that "there's no way we can possibly turn over our inventory 8 times in a year" find themselves at 22 annual inventory turns, hope to go higher, and "know" that they will do so.

The challenge in this mythical city is like playing a very sophisticated game of Monopoly. The mission, however, is not to "pass Go and collect $200" but to arrive simultaneously at Glastonbury and Avalon, to build a city beyond that of business-as-usual drudgery into one with greater purpose and, almost certainly, greater profits.

Glastonbury thinking is incapable of transforming the contextual rules of its own game. It only knows how to modify by increments its existing relationships regarding *things* like turf, silos, and functionalism, and *qualities* such as fear of speaking out, mistrust of others, need to control, destructive competition, resentment, and desire to look good. Glastonbury is able to generate more or less of what is already present—business as usual—but not to alter the context fundamentally. This sea change calls for the between, which belongs to Avalon. Glastonbury thinking cannot foster culture change because, of itself, it is unconscious of Avalon.

Changing Contexts

W. Edwards Deming, an American prophet originally unheard at home, tried unsuccessfully to introduce the idea of total quality management to the United States in the late 1940s. Japan, however, enthusiastically adopted his theories, and to this some experts attribute its spectacular recovery and success after World War II. Eventually, Deming's philosophy, summarized in *Out of the Crisis* (1991), was also adopted in America, and he was recognized as a hero by the country that originally rejected his vision.

Deming was insightful in telling executives that they should eliminate fear in the workplace and encourage joy in work. However, leaders who understand the importance of relationships conceptually but live their lives entirely in Glastonbury cannot follow his advice, because they actually view people as objective instruments in service of the organization's purpose. While such executives often adopted his procedural techniques for process improvement in detail, they were puzzled when their companies failed to transform.

Deming's suggestions for improving the on-the-job ambience included eliminating the annual performance appraisal and reducing competition among suppliers; he also encouraged education and training for all employees. While useful, however, these actions alone are insufficient to erase the cultural underpinnings of fear and mistrust that grow from the objectification of people, the natural corollary of Glastonbury. If the objectification continues, so will an underlying attitude of fear and mistrust, regardless of the formal and verbal reward practices. Corporate culture change happens in an organization only when Arthur and the entire leadership enter Avalon together to create the necessary cultural transformation from within its consciousness.

Culture change skills and techniques can be learned and applied, but only from within Avalon. Techniques that can work magic there usually fail miserably in Glastonbury. Indeed, such relational techniques, if not carried out in Avalon consciousness, may even prove destructive to the production and services Glastonbury offers.

Consider the game of chess as a *context*. First, it is important to remember that the generic game of chess is not the same as the specific one I played with my son yesterday. The former comprises an independent set of rules, regulations, and assumptions that lets anyone play and an underlying structure that provides the context for every particular game played. In agreeing to play by the rules of chess, the players agree to act and make choices within that context. Without it, there can be no game. On the other hand, the context of chess does not disappear when people don't play, and it wouldn't disappear even if no one played chess for 20 years. The rules are independent of any particular game of chess.

People new to any game either know the rules in advance or learn them as fast as possible. Similarly, anyone who goes through Marine boot camp finds out how to be a marine and either emerges as one or returns to the civilian world. Context is absolute. To change the context is to change the game. We are used to changing contexts where it doesn't matter much to us. On a family holiday, we may change from checkers to chess, from Monopoly to Parcheesi™, from poker to pinochle, or we may go outdoors and play baseball, followed by volleyball, table tennis, or shuffleboard. Each game has its unique context.

In parlor games or organized sports, we can easily shift contexts. In a business, where the leaders care deeply and have survived and succeeded within a set of practices and beliefs, changing context can be as hard as overcoming an addiction. Every action and choice happens in the existing—but usually transparent—context. Rules and assumptions are not as obvious as they are in a parlor game, but they operate nonetheless, and anyone who fails to respect them is in trouble.

I've watched dozens of companies try to train, manage, lead, reorganize, and downsize their way out of a constricting context. They do not succeed, however, because the fundamental rules do not change. The companies keep trying to fix something that isn't functioning within an existing set of rules instead of starting from a different set of rules. The latter can only come from an imagined and invented future. Historical contexts will not allow truly new sets of rules.

The Commerce Department will always create something that looks like the Commerce Department. Glastonbury can only create Glastonbury— even when it is as effective an example as Disney World. To reach Camelot, Avalon must also be incorporated.

2 MERLIN

Merlin is the messenger. His mission is to bring harmony to conflicting peoples. Through enchantment, argument and good sense he decodes a universal message in language that all women and men can hear. He represents the possibility of what it means to be human.

—Jack Schwarz, Founder and President
The Aletheia Health, Education, Assessment,
Relaxation, and Training Institute (Ashland, Oregon)[6]

erlin, Arthur's teacher, friend, and partner, guides the king in how to lead from Glastonbury and Avalon at the same time. Traditionally, Merlin is master of oblique shafts of insight and illumination, a warrior, wizard, trickster, spirit guide, detective, recluse, lover, logician, enchanter, madman, genius, manipulator, hypnotist, poet, holy person, and a defender both of free

[6]Personal communication, 1995.

thinking and of the kingdom. While Merlin is my hero and metaphor, I am hard pressed to find all of these qualities in myself or in any one of my colleagues.

Merlin in these pages, therefore, is a composite, a role to which one can aspire to help people fulfill themselves and their visions for their organizations. The legendary Merlin is, among other things, a potent example of what is possible when one person is totally dedicated to the success of another, as Merlin was to Arthur. This pattern can also work wonders in today's corporate world.

-+━

THE SWORD IN THE SOUP

In legend, when young Arthur drew the great sword Excalibur from the stone, he thereby proved he was the true king of Britain. But the days when disputes could be settled without remorse, with noble purpose, and with a mace are gone—and although I can sigh for those romantic times, we are probably well over them. But, no matter, I was born in this time, and in my story Excalibur rests not in the stone but in the soup—to be specific, Campbell's soup.

Merlin and Arthur's potential for powerful interaction was recently realized in a Canadian context. When C. David Clark became chairman and chief executive officer of Campbell Soup, Canada, in 1983, he made the company enormously successful by his nation's standards. Sales rose dramatically in the next four years. Its stock had doubled by 1989; its market share was rising; and the company had an aggressive new products track record. From 1987 to 1989, however, Clark worked in Europe for the company, returning home in 1989 to take once again charge of what he thought was a successful packaged-goods company, rightly perceived as a winner. When the U.S.-Canadian trade agreement passed that same year, however, this picture suddenly changed.

The parent corporation's new chief executive officer looked at competitive success entirely on North American terms, and Canadian management was dismayed to find out that its four plants were 25 to 40 percent less efficient than Campbell Soup's American counterparts. The message to the Canadian plants was clear: Close the gap, or close the plants.

At the present rate, Clark and his management team recognized, there would be no Canadian Campbell manufacturing plants within three years. Excellent incremental improvement would not be enough, but nobody in the company knew how to achieve the desired results. Two years later, however, Campbell had assured the continuance of its two major Canadian plants and had become a regional center, which, potentially, could send more than 50 percent of its goods to the United States. (In contrast, after the agreements, the Canadian packaged-goods industry as a whole experienced a significant loss of jobs, and some companies closed their plants.)

At Campbell, nine cross-functional teams had pledged themselves to produce a $9 million improvement in fiscal 1991 and achieved $26 million in annualized savings with a $16 million dollar impact in the first year. Share earnings grew by 30 percent in the face of a 3 percent decline in volume. In five months alone, due to the efforts of the cross-functional teams, $750,000 of pretax profit had been added. Employees from all levels, functions, and business units championed and supported the changes, working together to produce quantum results. The impact of a radically changed way of relating to one another on real work was palpable.

Said one worker, "Before, we put two-inch broccoli in one product and half-inch broccoli in another. Using only the small pieces in both products saved an enormous amount of money. Working with people in a new way has really moved us forward. You don't mind saying the things you were always afraid to say, and we've solved problems we never even used to discuss." A plant manager more than agreed:

The personal experience for me as a leader and a person has been overwhelming beyond anything in my life. I marvel at what I'm learning about myself and about other people. Our group beat the first $100,000 cost-saving goal by at least two and a half times. And we are looking at projects that will give us $15 million over the next 18 months.

What happened?

The story of Campbell, Canada, like most narratives, seems clear only through hindsight. In retrospect, a linear sequence of events produced a set of outstanding results. The past really does seem logical and comprehensible in a way that neither the present nor, certainly, the future does, despite how much we try to control them. Jean-Paul Sartre's belief that the perfect moment can only be remembered (not experienced) is correct (1974/1938). The past seems to exist in linear time—as an artistic recapitulation of what actually happened, in moment after successive moment—while the future exists as uncertainty, a promise of one successive risk after another.

At Campbell, Canada, hardly anything happened simply and straightforwardly. Initially, there was no agreement about the vision, and three vice presidents resigned in disaffection with the process and uncertainty about the company's future. (One, however, rejoined the company after a brief period.) Senior managers anticipated resistance from people at lower levels and avoided straightforward communication in direct proportion to the size of the group they had to face.

Merlin meetings, nearly always focused on identifying problems and obstacles to be engaged, rarely ended with a sense of satisfaction. All of the conclusive work was done by the Campbell management team *between* consultant sessions, in response to problems and obstacles that were revealed during the sessions themselves. After two years, Campbell, Canada, had succeeded.

The process, which had worked so well, seemed—in retrospect—simple, coherent, and appealing.

In reality, however, any explanation of organizational change is suspect. When a theory is used a second time, it falls short, because it lacks the power of the original invention. For example, a teacher in a poor neighborhood school found orange crates for the children to play with. Spontaneously, they piled the crates on top of one another, put the teacher's metronome on top, and, magically, they had "invented" a grandfather clock.

The delighted children pleased not only themselves but also the school principal, who looked in through the door and had the rare experience of seeing education happen before her eyes. She immediately went out and bought orange crates for all the classrooms, in the hope that the magic would happen everywhere. It didn't. Without spontaneous invention, orange crates are orange crates.

Great successes in organizational development are created through combinations of constancy of purpose, honesty, and spontaneous coinvention. A successful response to problems is rooted in commitment and loyalty, rather than self-justification or defense of someone's technical approach to development. The Campbell story is a testament to:
- Clark's leadership.
- most employees and managers' willingness to join together to coinvent an unpredictable future.
- the Merlin-Arthur relationship.

MERLIN AND ARTHUR

David Clark showed himself as Arthur early in our meetings. Normally, I hope to find Arthurian characteristics already present, because they predict a successful organizational change and a less stressful relationship. If the chief executive officer has none of these qualities, I usually give up. If some qualities are there and some are not, it is often possible to succeed largely out of Merlin's energy and commitment to Arthur's development.

━┿━

QUESTIONS FOR AFFIRMATION

If the answer is positive to at least half of the following questions, which I try to ask during our initial interview, Arthur has a chance of helping the company. This encounter serves as a dual test: S/he tries to decide whether I am credible; I probe to determine whether our partnership could work.

1. *Am I inspired by talking to this person?*
   S/he need not speak with the eloquence and certainty of a John F. Kennedy or a Golda Meir. S/he may be quiet and understated. But I sense inspiration if it is there.

2. *Do I sense strong energy coming from him/her?*
   This can be the energy of partnership in the making, or a sign that the relationship is star-crossed. The Merlin-Arthur connection becomes real when both believe in it. Clients and consultants who avoid the potential for uncertainty or responsibility in this relationship never see it.

3. *Does Arthur explicitly acknowledge his/her own uncertainty and stuckness?*
   When an executive "already knows," and "already has problems handled," or is "already doing that," or "has already done training like that," it's best to wish them luck and go home.

4. *Does Arthur struggle with questions thoughtfully?*
   If s/he isn't a self-generating champion of ideas, consultants will have to provide the necessary energy—a tedious procedure that does not produce self-sustaining change.

5. *Can Arthur think abstractly?*
   I always hope that the first questions are not about process but about the ideas or questions that generate it.

6. *Is Arthur explicit about time frames?*
   Does s/he immediately put work and results into a schedule? Does s/he show up on time or cancel meetings frequently? When Arthur's relationship to time is murky, it predicts an uncertain future.

7. *Am I confident, from the way Arthur talks, that the aim is for a world-class organization?*
   If s/he is willing to settle for less, that's what will follow.

When Clark asked us to facilitate the cultural and business transformation of Campbell Soup of Canada, we became more committed to his intentions than was Clark himself. An inquiry-based partnership developed immediately, and we unearthed what was best for customers, teams, and the company. Our commitment was to Arthur's consciousness, awareness of himself, values, team, company, and beyond—a commitment virtually without boundaries. Only Clark's own ability to think, feel, and react could limit the change effort. His ability to mirror the entire scene allowed him to mobilize people, materials, work, and services into a convincing Round Table and an inspired intent.

Merlin's intentions are irrelevant because his work context is always what Arthur and the knights' want and need. On one occasion, years ago, my vision for a client organization was stronger than its own for itself. Nonetheless, I managed to sell the organization on my ideas' validity. The results: A weak outcome and a dwindling relationship. Whenever one's own methodology, values, needs, or compulsions become the frame of the picture, Merlin's impact diminishes, replaced by self-serving rhetoric in the guise of contribution. Eventually Merlin disappears altogether from the system. One of the most powerful training technologies I know loses most of its audience because its authors ultimately care more about their own commitments and ideas than about the people to whom they are talking. In contrast, authentic partnership, based in true alignment and shared intention, provides a seamless, wholesome way to produce results without the suppressive effects of command and control leadership.

WHAT MERLIN ISN'T

Merlin is not a leader. Leadership is Arthur's job. And Merlin does not take action: Only Arthur and the knights can act credibly to change their situation. Neither does Merlin have to be present much. Often, the best changes happen when Merlin isn't there. And Merlin doesn't give advice, which can be useful and often necessary, but not the basis of magic. That results from the partnership itself and the mutual quest that precedes it.

Ultimately, Merlin never bests Arthur's ability to operate successfully in contradictory circumstances. As Arthur's consciousness grows, so does Merlin's. When Arthur reaches a personal or organizational bridge his knights will not cross, Merlin pauses in the same place. As in a good marriage, it becomes increasingly difficult to attribute success or failure to one party or the other. The whole becomes greater than the sum of its parts. Arthur's transformation flows *both* from Merlin's commitment and magic *and* the king's desire to promote Glastonbury results and Avalon cultural changes in the way people relate to each other.

+≔

MERLIN'S ROLE

The Shattered Mirror

In *Steppenwolf* (1928/1963), Hermann Hesse's hero finds himself standing in front of a shattered mirror. Every time the man moves, he is faced with a different image. They are all he, and they are all different. This vision parallels Merlin's view of a company, which always looks different depending on where the viewer is standing. At best, his shifting perspectives give him the ability to help Arthur alter his current ways of thinking and seeing the world. At worst, Merlin may find himself accused of cognitive slippage. In such an instance, while events make sense to Merlin, others think that several steps have dropped out of what otherwise would be a logical process.

Nothing upsets some people more than examining their own points of view. What separates Arthur from others is his interest and willingness to examine his point of view from outside. He is able to recognize that consciousness is housed and limited by fundamental points of view.

Campbell Soup of Canada had been operating from within assumptions common to most organizations, including the following:
- ⬥ Change is incremental.
- ⬥ Analysis is the basis of action.
- ⬥ Leaders should not be vulnerable in a dispute.
- ⬥ Responsibility for a company's success resides at the top.
- ⬥ Suppliers could not be expected to reduce their own prices dramatically.
- ⬥ Relationships, while important, merely happen and are not subject to management.
- ⬥ Agreement among executives has to come before the decision to act.
- ⬥ Employees only promise what they can predict.

Through a number of Merlin dialogues, Clark and his company came to see themselves in the magician's shattered mirror. Company personnel also began to look at the business from different points of view—all wholly or partially true and usually complementary. Said Hesse, "In every truth, the opposite is equally true." Campbell staff and executives came to see a parallel reality in which:
- ⬥ Step-order (that is, sudden, discontinuous, abrupt) change is a commonplace phenomenon.
- ⬥ Relationship is the basis of action.
- ⬥ Leaders gain power from their own vulnerability in a dispute.
- ⬥ Responsibility for the success of the entire company resides anywhere it is affirmed.
- ⬥ Suppliers can choose to join an effort to reduce their own prices.
- ⬥ Relationships can be deliberately improved.
- ⬥ Shared intention among key executives is the basis of extraordinary action.
- ⬥ Many employees will promise what they cannot predict.

Clark and his colleagues discovered their future in the questions we raised. When Merlin's shattered mirror fragments Arthur and the knights' attachment to their certainties, members of the organization come to practice a kind of contrary thinking that holds all assumptions up to scrutiny. At Campbell, Canada, the effects were a new culture and previously impossible results.

The Truth Teller

The Old Testament prophets like Isaiah and Jeremiah—as well as those of ancient Greece like Cassandra and Teiresias—were profound truth tellers. Such prophets, often without honor in their own countries, can find themselves in trouble when the truths they utter are unpopular. Those who reject the prophets' truth, however, close themselves to true freedom and healing.

Even in a folktale such as *Pinocchio*, the importance of telling the truth and acting honorably is an essential part of the message. Disney's film version emphasizes that moral with the invention of Jiminy Cricket, who serves as the wooden boy's conscience and who has the difficult job of keeping the puppet from lying and taking the easy way out. From Geppetto to the blue fairy to team builders, everyone seems to know that telling the truth is a fine idea. Who would say the truth is a bad idea? Imagine someone saying, "The truth? Bah, humbug. I hate the truth. What we need in this company is more lies and deceit." Still, when I ask people what stands in the way of real candor among them, they produce similar lists of concerns:

- If I do, I may get hurt.
- Things may get out of control.
- It's not that important anyway.
- I don't like to hurt other people.
- I'm afraid.
- "They" don't deserve it: "It's" not my problem.
- The way "they" are, the truth would never make a difference.
- I tell the truth, but not in groups.
- I tell the truth, but "they" don't listen.
- I will look bad.
- "They" will use the information I give to control me.
- Honesty would be a sign of weakness.
- He's a man, she's a woman; therefore, "they" wouldn't understand.

The reasons people give for dissembling are pervasive and powerful, and the truth often remains hidden, regardless of posted core values and even personal beliefs.

To Merlin, truth is unarguable because it is always uniquely person-al; it concerns only one's own experience, never anyone else's. Merlin carefully says, "*I am*," "*I want*," "*I see*," "*I hear*," "*I like*," and "*I don't like*." People feel attacked when confronted with an accusation that some-thing is wrong with them, but not when they hear a personal truth. When one's statement is resisted, the reason is often that s/he is not uttering personal truth, but offering criticism, even in disguise. When someone asserts that "this is the Truth," the implication is that no one should disagree. If one feels compelled to respond differently, s/he is asserting that "this" wasn't the "Truth" for him or her.

In showing corporate executives that truth (not Truth) is profound-ly personal, Merlin brings Arthur and the knights intellectually, emo-tionally, and spiritually beyond their sphere of comfort. At this point, the consulting contract is often in jeopardy. Herein lies the difference between Merlin and many other consultants, who attempt to keep their clients happy at all costs. Merlin, committed to Jiminy Cricket's conscientious work for his partners' success, is willing to lose the con-tract rather than lie. In the spirit of truth telling, Merlin wrote the fol-lowing letter to the president of a client company:

> I am writing this out of my commitment to you, to your company and to my own integrity.
>
> I see you as intelligent, competent, inquisitive, and generous. I rec-ognize fully the success and change you've created in the business. I respect your accomplishments, and I know that, with regard to running a successful business, I have a great deal to learn from you.
>
> But one situation is troubling to me and many others with whom I have talked in the company. I fear this difficulty may not resolve; however, if it does, the result could be—at best—even greater productivity and—at worst—peace of mind and satisfaction for a lot of people.
>
> Frankly, it sounds as if you won't allow anything to go on that you don't think you will ultimately be able to control. The effect is that

people feel dominated and suppressed, even when what you are saying is very useful. In addition, you always analyze before committing and thereby preclude one whole area of energy, possibility, and outcome.

You are not experienced as a counselor, but as a boss. As a counselor, however, you would achieve your goals. You would be surrounded with magnificent teams in the management committee, and—actually—you would end up with far more control than you have now. As a boss, you are operating within the limits of what you will or will not allow. Should you also function as a counselor, a coach, your staff could know *why* they are acting, take responsibility for their own decisions, keep going beyond their own limits, and be grateful to you.

I like you and want your years before retirement to be full of widespread acknowledgment of business success. The question is whether or not you're willing to stop dominating enough to empower people. To do so, I realize, will require a step-order change on your part—a quantum leap forward in your intentions and behavior. *You would have to be willing for people to make choices without your approval.* (Of course, their empowerment would not preclude your participation and ultimate, but more transparent, approval.)

For example, producing the extraordinary is not, essentially, an analytical process but one in which a team of people commit to producing a result—actual change in performance or organization. Such a project, by its very nature, is conducive to uncharacteristic action outside of "business as usual" and, therefore, is sometimes disconcerting.

If you *as boss* insist that the outcome be simply analysis, or, if you exercise your potential veto, you will alter what could be an extraordinary project into an incremental exercise whose major energy is focused on assuring your continuing support. If you squelch team commitment, the team is apt to fail, and the only future your company will achieve is the one you want and think is sensible.

Everyone I know in the company respects you, but, although you may not realize it, everyone on the management committee and many elsewhere feel you have them over a barrel which only you control.

I don't think you intend these effects. I expect that you think you are simply doing the right thing for the company. But the price in both human and business terms is high, although the success of parts of the business masks the overall loss of possibility and improvement in the company as a whole.

If you want to change this situation, I will be your full partner and devote myself to helping you. If you don't want to change the situation—or if you deny its existence or are able to justify it—then all I can do is the best I can. But if I am accurate and the condition persists, you will ensure that the company has an internal conflict in senior management philosophy that won't be resolved until you retire.

I am committed to you and the company in either case. What will be lost if you choose the second option is the opportunity for shared success.

Thanks for reading this.

Standing in front of the mailbox, Merlin balanced the relative importance of money and truth and mailed the letter. As it dropped, he briefly feared loss—both of revenue and of independence. For Merlin, the truth is a calling. Writes Annie Dillard in *Teaching a Stone to Talk*:

> The thing is to stalk your calling in a certain skilled and supple way, to locate the most tender and live spot and plug into that pulse. This is yielding and not fighting. The weasel does not "attack" anything: The weasel lives as he is meant to, yielding at every moment to the perfect freedom of single necessity. (1982, p. 18)

Merlin stalks the truth in Annie Dillard's sense—even when its dictates may turn business away.

Columbo

I've always admired the television detective Columbo played by Peter Falk because he, like Merlin, is so untidy and at the same time so effective. I don't trust tidy management consultants. According to Gregory Bateson, the basic distinction in science is between tidy and not tidy (1972). Everyone has an individual opinion about where that difference begins and ends.

Tidy consultants lay claim to linear, orderly company realities, which Merlin knows are valuable but only half true. He lives and works in companies that are half accurate and half mad, and his job is to help others *integrate* these potentially fruitful qualities, not simply to *analyze* and *organize* them.

Falk's well-played Columbo is a great detective who always gets his man or woman in an entertaining hour-long episode. Absolutely focused but apparently going nowhere, he shows up consistently at unexpected times, always looks disheveled, and brings an oblique challenge to whatever the usually well-heeled and spiffy client (suspect) is saying. Columbo collects his evidence, processes it, and intrudes persistently to reveal it at precisely the right moment. He takes personal interest in what people do and who they are, appreciating them in spite of the murders many of them commit. His stories about his wife and his dog, which seem to personalize the relationship between suspect and detective, are designed to irritate and disarm whoever he is investigating. A master of the art of inquiry, Columbo leaving often turns uncertainly and scratches his head to ask the "just one more question" that surprises the suspect with an unwelcome discovery.

Like Columbo, Merlin sees a world of chaos masquerading as order; like the detective, he compromises flexibly to reach his goal. The ability to make the most of imperfect circumstances is not helpful only for television detectives. To help executives succeed at unpredictable cultural and business transformations often requires Merlin to start over and over, sometimes, apparently, from the wrong places. Because Merlin, like Columbo, is willing to be uncertain, untidy, and unpredictable while maintaining an unerring commitment to the result, he usually gets the job done—handily, if often unconventionally.

Pogo

I have sworn upon the altar of God eternal hostility against every form of tyranny over the mind of man.

—*Thomas Jefferson,* 1800

The tyrannies against which Mr. Jefferson fought continue to thwart most cultural and business transformations. A true tyrant, however, is not necessary to make many people feel like victims. Just being an employee often does the trick—no matter what the boss does. By the same token, just being a boss makes many executives feel victimized by burdensome responsibility. In both cases, the state can seem endless.

It ain't necessarily so. Pogo said, "We have met the enemy, and they is us," and Merlin buys his statement. Merlin's job is to replace victimhood and tyranny and call people, instead, to heroism. At the outset of the Campbell, Canada, project, many people at all levels felt victimized by lack of:
- common vision in senior management.
- shared values among levels in the company.
- focused business commitment.
- information about where the company was going.
- team play.
- ability to close on strategic issues.

In addition, they struggled with:
- a culture that resisted measurement.
- authoritarian behavior.

- archaic processes.
- individual preconceptions based on prior success or failure.

And their difficulties were compounded by the contradictory tugs of:
- bottom-line people versus soft-process people.
- not enough collective thinking versus too much collective thinking.
- suspicious people versus insecure people.
- people who can fire you versus people you can't fire.
- having too low standards versus having too high standards.

After two years, however, tens of thousands of acts of individual and team heroism had contributed to the company's cultural and business transformation. Complaints had turned to constructive attitudes and activities, and different procedures, over time, produced remarkable synergy and results. Each time individuals caught themselves playing victim to each other, to corporate headquarters, or to their existing processes, they consciously pulled themselves up short.

On the other side, Campbell, Canada found freedom, pride of accomplishment, and much increased productivity.

The Healer

In our productivity-driven corporate cultures, the term "healer" seems out of step, conjuring pictures of personal growth gurus and teachers of obscure mystical disciplines. In recent years, a number of such people have earned our suspicion. We question whether they care for us or for our money. We challenge the efficacy of their methods, especially when their prices are high. Their own lives often seem to belie their philosophies.

I used to characterize such healing as a transformational car wash, which promises to resolve one's deepest concerns and make one's fondest dreams come true. After providing a positive healing experience, however, the already converted washers note that, "Oops, we forgot to tell you, the car only stays clean if you participate in our ongoing transformation program, follow our diet, worship according to our religion, take our vitamins, and come in for a weekly wash forever."

Eventually, I came to see that—while it's true that developing and changing always requires practice—the promise of fundamental improvement is both usually false and also alters the context of the buyer-seller relationship from healing to sales, marketing, and code-pendence. Instead of finding oneself in heaven, one finds oneself in a department store.

In spite of these pitfalls, Merlin is indeed a healer. He does not so identify himself, however, any more than he says he is Pogo or a shattered mirror. Merlin's context is determined by what the client wants, which is always business centered, even when it takes the form of cultural and human concerns. To Merlin, healing, enlivening, and making a business hearty is, like the truth, more important than money. Every corporation bears scars and is continuously wounding and being wounded.

Arthur's imperative is to create a first-rate organization through the world-class partnership of the Round Table. Merlin's goal is to heal in the context of a client's business interests. The imperative to heal, more important than getting more business, more important even than survival, provides the context through which Merlin fulfills his own destiny. Whether the healing is most fundamentally derived from the cost reduction that originates in Glastonbury or the compassionate listening that starts in Avalon, it is the fabric of Merlin's intentions.

Deep in the origins of various Anglo-Saxon languages is a word-root *hal*. From it, we derive a number of words used in contemporary English:

- *hale*, as in full of energy.
- *health*, as in well-being, growth, and development.
- *heal*, as in recovering from a wound or mending divisions.
- *(w)hole*, as in wholeness, holistic, united, or unified.
- *holy*, as in sacred, to be treated with reverence and care.

Merlin must first heal himself, looking after his own energy, brushing away that which would drain it, and avoiding negative energy. He constantly faces the obstacles—within and without himself—to healing the business and the people in it. In *The Crystal Cave*, Merlin said: "The Gods only go with you if you put yourself in their path. And that takes courage" (Stewart, 1980, p. 55).

When I look at Arthur or a knight, I often see in them what I am afraid of or reject in myself. This recognition is the entrance to the place of my own healing, as well as of theirs and of their company. Here, magic lives, and organizational and personal energies, once suppressed, take voice. From this dark spring, Campbell Soup of Canada saved its manufacturing plants, began to heal its relationship with its corporate parent, and, producing extraordinary Glastonbury results from a company-wide Avalon, began to experience Camelot.

3 THE ARTHURIAN IMPERATIVE

he Arthurian imperative in business is the intent to create a Round Table of colleagues and employees aligned in service of a shared heartfelt purpose, which can be as basic as making money legally or as ambitious as becoming the best food company in North America. The goal can be as noble as bringing peace to the Middle East or as practical as providing the best quality service to diesel engine distributors worldwide.

Men and women who embody the Arthurian imperative are driven, for reasons they do not always understand, to align people's intelligence and energies in strategic intent and to unify from a morass of turfdoms a corporate kingdom. The role of Arthur is usually not consciously chosen; it is affirmed as destiny or quest.

The Arthurian imperative is not a calling that automatically resides in a company's chief executive. Anyone at any level can have it. When the senior person in a hierarchy has or aspires to the Arthurian imperative, a brighter future seems possible. The imperative itself, however, must create its extraordinary business success through the aligned organization of a Round Table. Whoever embraces the imperative is willing to take on whatever is in the way including—most importantly—oneself. Therein lies the rub. Creating a two-person partnership is plenty difficult, but building and maintaining a Round Table of established knights is even more challenging. For most corporate executives, blinded by the glitter of the successes they believe have come, ultimately, from their own efforts, even the idea of an aligned company is unthinkable.

The journey to the Round Table demands the strength to face demons and dragons, initiations and joys. Arthur must be able to defy conventional wisdom, to see what is there, not what s/he expects. Zukav points out in his "overview of the new physics" that researchers in quantum physics looking for a particle find a particle; those looking for a wave find a wave (*The Dancing Wu Li Masters*, [1979/1984]). As Ellen Gilchrist notes, however, *Light Can Be Both Wave and Particle* (1989).

One has a tendency to find that for which one searches. Someone seeking to revitalize an organization from a Glastonbury point of view sees Glastonbury; those looking to reform Avalon will see Avalon. In attempting to build a Round Table, Arthur looks to something new—a corporate Camelot where people do quality work and make money in Glastonbury while relating to others from Avalon.

What is increasingly clear, however, is that a company that captures both people's hearts and minds flows from the way the leadership relates to it. Conventional wisdom is not enough to make a difference here. People do not seem to get along much better than they did hundreds or possibly thousands of years ago. Building a Round Table in organizations offers little real hope without a breakthrough in the way leaders see the world.

To be a successful corporate leader, Arthur must be grounded in conventional, time-tested Glastonbury beliefs. For much of history, they have been the accepted bases of success both for business itself and for achieving senior leadership positions. Captains of industry, robber barons, and financially successful industrial executives have offered public proof that business is really a matter of deciding how much to sell, determining how to sell it, and organizing people decisively around these two ends. The corporate Arthur has been such a businessperson whose life and career bear witness to the following Glastonbury beliefs:

1. The corporation is a visible, physical, real, and measurable entity. What you see is what you get.
2. Wealth comes from effort, action, productivity, and good business practices—making good decisions and acting effectively.
3. If one demands short-term quantifiable results, employees, given enough encouragement and monetary incentive, will produce them.
4. Money comes from money-making activities.
5. Authority comes from power, control, or expertise. The ability to influence the actions of others definitively comes, in great part, from one's position or role in the organization.
6. Good procedures provide good solutions: Analysis leads to action, and action produces results.
7. Results produce the future. The organization's future arises from the organization's past and present successes.

These principles are at work in most successful companies, and control of important organizational resources usually goes to people whose actions are guided by these assumptions. If, however, Arthur is seeking fundamentally to change the way a business operates in an era of confounding economic, social, and technological complexity, he revolutionizes these principles by pioneering a perspective that combines what is known of the best of Glastonbury with the best of Avalon.

The following principles are an attempt to articulate this new perspective.

+⊨≡

PRINCIPLES FOR THE ROUND TABLE

The Organization Is the Response of Its Leadership

A company does not exist objectively. The moment-to-moment response of Arthur and the knights shapes reality for the entire organization. The impact of this principle is profound and pervasive but not obvious. A corollary is equally provocative: To alter fundamentally or revitalize an organization, one must change the way its leadership responds to it.

I don't play tennis, mostly because—as a kid—I chased tennis balls for more experienced players and found the experience tedious and embarrassing. Thus, it was without enthusiasm that I recently attended a workshop based on W. Timothy Gallwey's *Inner Game of Tennis* (1974) with a client company's senior management. As I stood on the court, racquet in hand, my comfort level was low. As the trainer hit the ball toward me, it was supposed to bounce once, and I was to hit it back. As it bounced, I was to say, "Bounce"; as I hit it, I was to say, "Hit."

This apparently simple charge was not as easy to fulfill as it seemed. I often said "bounce" too early or late, and I sometimes said "hit" before or after the moment of impact. With practice, my timing improved. So did that of the other participants. As we neared our goal of simultaneously speaking and acting, we discovered to our surprise that, for rank amateurs, we were actually volleying rather successfully. I felt like a different person playing a different game. The ball was now appearing in a way that allowed me to hit it.

Thereafter, whenever I failed to say the words at the exact moment of bounce or hit, I hit the ball ineffectively. The coincidence of naming and occurrence altered what actually happened. The reality was shaped by the observer's response. Through constant naming, both the harmony and the dissonance in the alignment between my plan and my action became clearly apparent.

The owner of a growing consulting firm jogging in London's Hyde Park and listening to a tape of Deepak Chopra (1994) extolling the power of intention to shape one's health and physical reality had a similar experience. The jogger, predisposed to believe the tape's message, said to himself, "I intend—and I always have—to build an aligned company of owners."

In spite of his hope, for years the senior employees of his firm had formed an uneasy alliance without partnership or unity with regard to business purposes, operating philosophy, management style, or customer service. In the weeks following that morning's run, however, the jogger began to exclaim equivalents to "bounce" and "hit" when opportunities to demonstrate ownership occurred and issues of alignment presented themselves. As time went on, organizational issues of alignment (and dissonance) clarified, and gradually the company shifted to become consistent with the naming.

Language has an inventive power. It shapes what happens.

Two months later, his company had moved into unity and alignment. Staff meetings changed from uncertain exercises in suppressed criticism and divisiveness into communicative, straightforward conversations. Consistent results took the place of inconclusive opinions. Spontaneous initiatives replaced unimaginative, archaic technical designs. Almost everyone suddenly found the company's old strategic plan unrealistic and took a new look at sales and profits.

And staff changes led to greater harmony and productiveness:
- One senior consultant, a talented star performer who never played on any team but his own, rejected an offer of partnership and resigned.
- The chief operating officer angrily resigned in the face of requirements that she deal with others more sensitively.
- An effective sales and marketing staffer appeared on the company doorstep.
- The formerly dedicated but uninspired controller became forward-looking, assertive, and creative.

↤ A previously mousy secretary started speaking out in meetings with the intelligence, impact, and energy of an expert.
↤ A mild-mannered consultant took charge of a major client with whom she began to do increasingly productive business.

The organizational reality had changed with the same clarity and immediacy as the occurrence of impact on tennis ball with the saying of "bounce" and "hit." Most staff, responding to new freedom with greater self expression, experienced a rush of confidence both in their future and that of the business.

The revitalized organization was the result of the leader's changed response to it.

Arthur's Intent Shapes Response

When one operates from intent, the world becomes simple and lucid. Annie Dillard, in referring to the "perfect freedom of single necessity," actually describes the singular power that follows when someone mentally and emotionally frees true intent from the concerns and attachments that muddy it. The immediate and dramatic effect of such clarified intent is a philosopher's stone that turns an organization's base metal into gold.

Simple but difficult intentions are a key to Arthur's kingdom. Clear directions do not assure easy processes, however; just because one knows the destination does not guarantee an easy journey. Most upsets and distractions come from frustrated intent, but most people do not even acknowledge their intentions, merely experiencing pain when they are thwarted. Identifying one's intentions and embracing them fully is the beginning of what Gordon Allport (1950/1970) defines as an integrated philosophy of life, a mark of a productive and mature person. A leader's intentions form the substance of his or her response, shaping, determining, and thereby creating the very organization.

Intention is a magnet in the relational world. Just as a magnet placed under a paper sprinkled with iron filings aligns all the filings into a coherent pattern, the magnetic energy of Arthur's intention meaningfully arranges the people in his or her organization. When Arthur's intention is clear and strong, it cuts through the Gordian knot of entangled communication, bureaucracy, and misunderstanding.

What s/he intends can be small (a successful meeting) or great (accomplishing the organization's singular, long-term strategic intent into concrete business actions like Honda's setting out to become a "second Ford," an intent that became reality 20 years later). Intent, which is often present and active though not always revealed, can operate in many everyday situations. For example, one may intend to spend time with one's family, to rest before strenuous activity, to become rich, . . . or to play Ping-Pong™ nonstop for three days.

That was the surprising accomplishment, two decades ago, of Esmail R. Karimi, a research project manager for Perkins International Limited (Peterborough, England). To raise funds for the Society for the Prevention of Cruelty to Children, Karimi forced himself to play table tennis with 125 people for 72 hours and 10 minutes.[7] Only a casual player before his marathon, Karimi broke the European record for nonstop Ping-Pong™.[8] His feat, the result of intention-shaping response in the face of an extraordinary challenge, stemmed from the same kind of conscious choice that drives all successful business leaders and entrepreneurs.

The impetus for Karimi's endurance record, astonishingly, originated in a chance remark. When a newspaper editor invited him to compete, Karimi laughed and casually promised her that he was game. Embarrassed to find his intention in print the next day, he protested to the editor, who said, fairly, that all she had done was publish what he had promised. "I'm sure you can do it," she added, a confidence Karimi did not originally share.

---

[7] Players were permitted five-minute rest breaks each hour.

[8] Unofficial, to be sure: Marathon table tennis events, amateur affairs conducted to raise money, do not receive formal recognition in the UK.

His intention, however shaky, had become public. Karimi considered dismissing it as a foolish mistake, but instead decided to claim it, and—in the few weeks before the competition—practiced diligently, mobilized a supporting team, and raised over £1,000 in 1974 (which translate to between $7,000 and $8,000 in 1995). Because most of his sponsors lacked his and the editor's optimism, they tended to volunteer substantial hourly amounts. His stamina cost them dear.

When Karimi claimed the intention to win as his own, his environment changed from a business-as-usual viewpoint to one that reflected confidence, perception, responsibility, and energy. He learned methods of staying awake, studied the reports on other marathon competitors, and found the chaos his promise had introduced increasingly organized by his intention to win, which turned the undoable into the possible into the triumphant.

Strategic Intent Shapes Collective Response

Just as a leader's intent shapes his or her response to the organization, an aligned intent among members of the organization at large also shapes their collective response. When such an intent is "strategic" in a business sense, it makes possible a new way to plan for the future that unleashes many of the shackles of the past.

When Gary Hamel and C. K. Prahalad (1989) analyzed the exceptional success of winning competitors in a number of industries, they started from an unusual perspective. Instead of using an analysis of current or projected conditions as a base for predicting success, they looked for the presence of a commitment to create a future that could *not* be reasonably extrapolated from the business's original state. This *"stretch commitment"* transformed the internal cultures of those corporations. (For more on the importance of stretch, see pages 103–107.)

Strategic intent envisions a desired leadership position and establishes the criterion the organization will use to chart its progress. Komatsu set out to "encircle Caterpillar," and did so. Canon successfully sought to "beat Xerox"; Honda, as we've mentioned, "to become a second Ford." All these slogans are expressions of strategic intent, and all of them were realized.

What changed when these companies adopted their strategic intents? Hamel and Prahalad report no tremors at Xerox headquarters the day that Canon's leadership declared its plan, and the marketplace was similarly unperturbed. The impact of the new strategic intent affected Canon's internal culture first, as people throughout the organization took personal responsibility for changing every aspect inconsistent with it. The extraordinary results flowing from these internal changes eventually rippled outward to transform the industrial pattern. Canon did come out first.

Through the process of aligning to strategic intent, leadership teams transform themselves and the culture of their organizations through creative commitment to a radically different future. *Leading from the premise of strategic intent requires one to think and plan backwards from that envisioned future in order to take effective action in the present.* An executive who enlists an organization in strategic intent continually reveals the desired future in the competitive opportunities of the present.

This process often starts with a personal vision of the organization's future that confronts the shared reality of its existing culture. As other members of the organization commit to this vision, it becomes an aligned strategic intent that shapes people's response to circumstances as they occur. For example, the National Aerospace Plane Program[9] has successfully designed an airplane that will fly 25 times the speed of sound (Mach 25), while taking off and landing from a runway rather than with boosts from multistage rockets. (The fastest commercial plane today flies around Mach 2.)

---

[9]Barthelemy's project was part of the joint program of several federal entities including the National Aeronautic and Space Administration and the U.S. Air Force, Navy, and Department of Defense.

Of this intent, then Program Director Robert ("Bart") Barthelemy wrote,

> Although the concept of aerospace planes routinely traveling from earth to space (as do subsonic airplanes from airport to airport) set the vision, it was clear to the early [Program] volunteers that more focus was required in order to develop the technology needed for such an airplane. . . .(1994, p. 21)

Later, Barthelemy reminisced,

> I became much more than myself when I took the goal of making an airplane fly at Mach 25 and made it my own. I was able to go beyond the limitations I had previously placed on myself as an individual. Things like that aircraft, which most people think impossible, become real because they're already there before you find the way to get to it. Things happen when you commit. That's the key. With commitment, a project takes on an aura of its own. (personal communication, 1995)

When Barthelemy originally talked about eliminating the distinction between earth and space, he released vast energy among almost thousands of people in many collaborating and competing companies and laboratories who formed an unlikely Round Table and, against formidable political and technical obstacles, developed the single-stage-to-orbit airplane. He summarized:

> Beginning with two people in 1985, the [Program] gained supporters by the dozens. By 1987, over 1,000 people were involved in the Program, industry was contributing over $100 million of their own research and development money to the effort, the five-agency government sponsoring group was delivering $150 million a year in funding, and people were leaving comfortable government and industrial jobs (I did) just to be part of the Program. . . .
>
> After two years of operation in this mode, the National Team, which includes the government as a partner, has made breakthrough progress. A new, synergistic single concept of the X-30

has emerged, and it incorporates the best ideas of all the companies and the government. All duplication has been eliminated and individuals from every organization are working on cross-company teams in very effective ways. Complete openness is the norm and the distinction between companies has almost disappeared. There is still competition, but it is competition of ideas and not organizations. (1994, pp. 41, 79)

The means to fulfill this strategic intent may be unknown or nonexistent when it is adopted. Neither Komatsu nor Honda knew how they would overtake their U.S. rivals, but win they did. When President Kennedy predicted in 1961 that the United States would put a man on the moon before 1970, no one was quite sure how this would happen—but it did! Similarly, although CocaCola™ didn't know how it would "put a Coke™ within arm's reach of everyone on the planet", it has moved powerfully in that direction.

In each case, commitment to the strategic intent preceded the development of the requisite methods for accomplishing it. *Acceptance of a future vision entailing a new set of beliefs about the identity and capability of the organization freed the creative thinking necessary to invent ways to achieve the strategic intent.* Arthurian leaders play a critical role in this process by consistently representing the strategic intent in an ongoing dialogue with the existing organizational culture. The leader attracts creative tension between the entrenched culture and the new strategic vision.

Once having stated a strategic intent, it becomes necessary to demonstrate practically to everyone that it is possible. Our study of several successful demonstrations of strategic initiatives showed each met the following criteria. Each:

- focused everyone in the organization on a single, specific, long-term objective.
- offered a deliverable product or service, not an idea.
- provided something customers really wanted.
- was possible, although the means to it were unknown.
- forced a global, not fragmented, point of view.
- could be borne out palpably in many ways—on charts, through

roll-out plans, through cooperative effort, in demonstrations to customers.

- ☞ transcended what the organization had achieved before.
- ☞ involved risk.
- ☞ furnished a beacon everyone could see.

If the initiative does not meet these criteria, there is a real possibility that the strategic intent won't serve either the organization or its most vital resource, the customer. In such cases, however, a powerful strategic initiative can foster a point of view that can unify the whole organization in terms that everyone can understand and apply to his or her work, regardless of position. IBM achieved such a focus in its Karat initiative, which worked to make previously incompatible computer software products function harmoniously. Karat eventually evolved into the company's enormously successful IBM SystemView.™

Wrote IBM Enterprise Management Vice President William E. Warner, Jr.,

> With Karat, we embraced the notion of going from 160 different products down to one, for our customers' ease of use. Our value statement promises to ship everything in one package.
>
> Karat became the first choice in managing a new world of possibilities. Our customers really want it. It's provided a single focus for the whole entity. It transcends what we can do ourselves, and it involves risk. It has caused people to think about marketing, planning, development, delivery, and distribution in ways they have never done before.
>
> And, when we began, we didn't know how to do it. That was the real challenge, the real glow in the lighthouse. To have permission to create is what gave this thing called Karat life. . . . Now, in most of the population at Enterprise Management, there's a little bit of Karat.
>
> IBM has the best brains in certain technology fields, and when we get our act together, we are hard to beat. That's what Karat represents. We have all of IBM working on the same problem, and that's pretty extraordinary.

Camelot: An Aligned Organization
Tuned to a Single Intelligence with Unlimited Energy

This principle in action underlies a test maneuver used in Marine basic training. Eleven marines are dropped into a hole in the ground eight-feet deep. The trainer throws a "live" hand grenade into the hole. For the men to scramble out safely in the 10 seconds before the grenade "explodes" requires an extraordinary amount of alignment, focused energy, trust, cooperation, and urgency. When the group's escape is successful, it appears that a single integrative intelligence has been working for 11 individuals. Similarly, a successful professional basketball team of 5 players seems to operate from one intelligence. The same is true for a symphony orchestra comprising 98 people performing a concert. Three thousand people in an electricity company acting as one to pass cost savings to its customers is another.

David Bohm (1980) argues that, contrary to our experience of thinking as an individual, isolated phenomenon, thinking is largely collective in nature. He goes on to stress the vital role of interactive dialogue if one is to harness the collective intelligence actually there. Such an alignment drove much of the National Aeronautics and Space Administration during the Apollo project to put a man on the moon by 1969 (within the decade President Kennedy had promised), even in the face of constant technical and organizational disputes.

In times of extensive alignment, many people experience almost limitless energy, aim for far-reaching goals, and find a pervasive sense of partnership, oneness, and shared confidence. They are often able to handle anything the future holds; resignation and cynicism disappear into team spirit. Fear of suppression disappears, and, in such times, people really love their company in both in a business and social sense.

Most of these moments do not last. The Apollo Project ended when men landed on the moon, and the National Aeronautics and Space Administration has suffered some painful and demoralizing defeats since that triumph. Company crises that pull people together end, and everyone goes back to business as usual. Training programs end, and the discipline that allowed work in Glastonbury to occur with the spirit and practices of Avalon dissolves in the "reality" of Monday morning.

Each burst of united energy seems generated by leadership committed to a Round Table, to revitalization, and to a shared and heartfelt goal. Maintaining this state is the Arthurian imperative. In its absence, the powerful energy available to an organization and the individuals in it is almost always suppressed.

Imagine what any organization could accomplish with 1,000 times its current energy. One version of the Arthurian legend says that it was when Merlin, whose own energy was prodigious, discovered 300 individuals in Britain with similar commitment and gathered them together in a bramble in Wales, Camelot emerged.[10] Corporate Avalon can join with Glastonbury to recreate Merlin's accomplishment in an organizational Camelot.

+═══

PARADIGMS FOR PARALYSIS

Knights Who Protect by Draining Energy from Others

I sat at the end of the table and watched the conversation spin. Someone shot down every good idea, as the group became increasingly demoralized. Suggestions for improvement were received with glazed eyes as people returned to whatever point they were trying to make in the first place.

The stakes were high. The company had downsized 25 percent in a few short years. Many of the best remaining people had jumped ship in favor of more promising opportunities. Those who were left worked hard to fight the recurrent depression that comes from not being able to see an inviting future—or even any future at all.

---

[10]Stuart Wilde makes use of the Arthurian quest on cassettes, *Camelot* (n.d.).

Still, it was and had been a great company. Its remaining members were among the brightest men and women with whom I had ever worked. Its ability to invent technology was incomparable, and its global distribution channels were the envy of its competitors. If this company sat as a Round Table, it would win individually and as a group.

But I was sure that they would never even be able to agree on what movie to see together, let alone how to proceed effectively with difficult cost reduction and critical process reengineering. Their pattern was clear and predictable as a clock's second hand ticking through the minutes of a day.

Their repetitive dance, punctuated by six steps, continued.

The pattern?

1. Someone suggests a promising, uncharacteristic *idea* for moving a process reengineering project forward.
2. The room fills with *hope*, enthusiasm, energy, a sense of possibility, and confidence in the future.
3. Almost immediately, someone feels *threatened* and engages in an automatic way of dealing with real or perceived danger.

In one instance, when a woman became afraid that a solution might make her lose power, look bad to her constituencies and to herself, and end with her subservient to other players, she at once became domineering and began to act as if she were being victimized. Changing tactics, she then offered a rational and penetrating interrogation of the arguments she feared, smothering the original suggestion in logic and leaving it limp and defenseless on the table.

Her domination was complete, and her response was far from unique. The tyrant in each of us, if unsuppressed, can lead us into fear-driven, self-righteous, aggressive action . . . or inaction. We are willing to withdraw from almost any relationship to protect our fundamental point of view and interests. Sometimes, its expression is blatant; sometimes it is hidden in someone whose soft-spoken generosity masks unwillingness to make real commitments.

4. An invisible force sucks the vitality out, as participants' permeates the room.

   People shrink slightly into their chairs. Because of business etiquette, their deflation is expressed through the quiet resignation the culture has substituted for human rage.

5. A brief period of further conversation, characterized by personal dissociation, superficiality, and *bright, animated pretense* follows.
6. The entire pattern *repeats* again as someone suggests an originally promising and uncharacteristic idea.

   Remarkably, this cycle spun three times during the meeting. When I noticed this, I diagrammed it on paper and showed it to the participants. They smiled sheepishly, acknowledged its truth, and went on repeating the process. Occasionally, I pointed out which step someone was on, and the group again smiled helplessly. They saw no way out. Every time someone avoided domination, didn't lose, tried to look good, sought to win, and achieved self-justification, more people's energy drained slowly away into a puddle of resignation.

   Once again, passengers rearranged their deck chairs on this corporate Titanic.

The Wounded King

Arthur, while a great leader is also a human being with human flaws. One corporate leader, for example, is a courageous risk taker and a brilliant analyst but also considers himself the pawn of his boards of directors and owners. As victim, he throws his Round Table into disarray.

Another ruler, a master speaker and creator of possibilities for others, is unwilling to fire anyone who has not totally infuriated her—something that almost everyone usually avoids. Instead of confronting and changing or terminating unacceptable (but not completely maddening) behavior, she tries to rise above it, becomes aloof, and pretends that everything is all right. Tense conversations become unauthentic and the business suffers. This aloofness undermines company alignment, and the prize remains close but elusive.

Still another is an imaginative dreamer and visionary. When questioned, however, he interrogates colleagues like the Gestapo, undermining the fledgling Round Table in his company and industry for which he is a major spokesperson.

A fourth, an uncanny economist and business genius, is also dominating, manipulative, and covert. The private game he plays brings significant success to certain business units but precludes a Round Table's synergy within the company as a whole.

In the face of threat, Arthur may put up a natural defense mechanism similar to others'. The Arthurian imperative requires an ongoing willingness to transcend this mechanism and, over time, to behave honestly and openly in spite of its dictates.

In the behavior of a corporate Arthur seeking to fulfill a great purpose and build a Round Table, the price otherwise is an enormous suppression of people's energy and the fragmentation of corporate alignment and relationship. Resignation takes its place, and people experience the demoralization that comes from knowing that they are not really partners after all.

The Arthurian imperative is a journey, and the leader's quest includes the conquest of his own natural defense mechanisms. Though they are more like a habit, such as a craving for chocolate, than a tumor to be excised or a demon to be slaughtered, Arthur knows that controlling them nonetheless requires vigilance. One doesn't have to eat chocolate, but, typically, the craving is often there. One *needn't* dominate, even though it may seem necessary at the first sign of conflict.

For Arthur to control a natural defense mechanism, he must exercise high-order discipline, vigilance, and consciousness. A leader building a Round Table, however, must be many faceted: The role requires the persistence of Sisyphus, the courage of Gawain, and the humor of Sancho Panza. In every case, the limits to the revitalization of the organization and growth of the Round Table are at personal bridges Arthur is reluctant to cross. Every time Arthur transcends his automatic response, a period of increased energy and surprising accomplishment radiates through his knights to the entire realm.

Mordred: When a Knight Goes Astray

Sometimes the mirrors are corrupt; sometimes the viewer is blind. Like Narcissus, Mordred (King Arthur's illegitimate son) never sees anyone in the mirror but himself. While Narcissus, in love with his own reflection, fell into the pond mirroring him and drowned, Mordred was not merely *self*-destructive. According to legend, he eventually led the forces that destroyed the Round Table and brought Camelot to dust, although faith burns that the wounded king will be healed and return in triumph from Avalon. Mordred, a jealous and wily fellow, had a finely honed ability to make use of the weaknesses in Arthur's character to turn others against him.

Mordred cared little for the kingdom or its people. What he did care about was himself. His deceit was seamless. With no chinks in his personal suit of armor, he consistently escaped responsibility for his actions. He made sure that his purpose appeared noble (and that Arthur's seemed tainted). Surrounding himself with toadies who never talked back and tolerating his supporters' unacceptable behavior because to forbid it would cast bad light on *him*, the king's son poisoned his father's kingdom.

Mordred can have a devastating effect on the Round Table. The corporate Arthur, like the legendary king, is often reluctant to deal decisively with an obviously misbehaving Mordred. Arthur's commitment to others' success and development makes him reluctant to take disciplinary action, and—sooner or later—instead of becoming unified, the company fragments. The velocity and accomplishment made possible by aligned leadership cannot be sustained, although Mordred may well succeed individually. One corporate Mordred clothed his action in the guise of responsible business judgment:

> I personally struggle now only with the chief executive officer, who is getting directly involved with my division. We cannot deal with the number of committees, initiatives, and paper flow his new way of thinking and running a business has created.
>
> My people are so confused, they're going around in circles. The top banana has lost control, in my humble opinion. Talk to all my guys and ask them directly, "Why isn't it any better?" There's no answer. I'm not running the business any longer, I have very little input in my own department now.
>
> In fact, the chief executive officer is more directly involved there than I am. What happens is, he ends up cutting guys like me out of the picture, and—if you were to go around and see every senior person in all of the separate divisions—you'd find a group with a lot more résumés on the street today than ever before. If the corporation disappeared tomorrow morning, we wouldn't miss a heartbeat. We would lose some valuable services, but we would replace those efficiently, and nothing would change.
>
> None of this gets resolved in the executive committee, because the boss doesn't listen. He didn't want to listen to me one-on-one, and he also dislikes talking to the managers in a group. I've told him that I don't agree with a lot of the things that are going on. I told him that, slowly but surely, his company and my company are diverging to a point where I'm going to have trouble identifying them. I don't necessarily have to be around for the long pull, but I think if I were to leave, it would send the wrong signals. To make it a short-time hurt for the company, I'd much rather leave after we've negotiated a timetable.

Is this knight really Mordred, or would better communication have resolved the situation? There is no certain answer and, in this case, the negative energy and cross-purposes persisted for years. Because Mordred's business results were the best in the company, the chief executive officer had a hard time simply removing him. The boss's attempts to make the situation developmental failed repeatedly: "I'm fine the way I am," said Mordred, but, eventually, he left on his own initiative.

An almost tangible sense of relief swept through the company. Finally, the knights could turn from a mirror that emphasized every wart. Facing a real problem (as opposed to considering a hypothetical one) often clarifies priorities. Without Mordred, Arthur and the knights had another chance to create Camelot.

⊬⊨

BECOMING ARTHUR

Arthur at his best mirrors the whole kingdom, reflecting its radiant energies. In turn, the kingdom mirrors the king. In this phenomenon, Camelot draws on more than simply Arthurian traditions. Parallels could be drawn reflecting elements of Far Eastern philosophies,[11] as well as the writings of Gottfried Wilhelm Leibniz (1646–1716).[12]

Changing the way a company fundamentally operates is as difficult as curing an addiction. Successes from programs designed primarily to achieve physical detoxification offer a paradigm for would-be corporate transformers. Alcoholics Anonymous's well-known 12-step program, for example, has been relatively successful in helping people stop drinking. Since many corporate personnel are as attached to their cultures as alcoholics to liquor, I have borrowed the 12-step approach from Alcoholics Anonymous to suggest a parallel program for organizational leaders who want to alter their companies' cultures.

---

[11]Stephen Levine and Ondrea Levine write, "Over the course of three million years, we were shaped in relation to the forces and cycles of the natural world; we are, in our most essential being, mirrors and dreams of the earth" (1995, p.86).

[12]According to Leibniz, the universe comprises countless conscious centers of spiritual energy called monads. Each one represents a microcosm that independently mirrors the perfection of the perfectly harmonious universe. That humankind's limited vision cannot generally appreciate a divine harmony that includes pain and suffering does not mean that that harmony does not exist. It only means that people are too limited to be able to recognize and comprehend it.

To become a successful leader for corporate change, Arthur must confront and resolve the following personal challenges:

1. Admit that you are personally unable to make the difference you want to make with the organization and that, without that change, the organization is becoming unmanageable.

2. Believe that a discipline consistent with your values, but unfamiliar, can bring you and the organization to a state of innovation, accomplishment, and well-being.

3. Accept the guidance of a partner who has mastered this discipline.

4. Make a searching inventory of your and the organization's record of keeping commitments, taking personal responsibility for results, and suspending beliefs for the sake of possibility.

5. Tell your partner and your work team exactly what isn't working and describe your vision for the organization and its people.

6. Be ready to attack defects in the organization's character—its values, beliefs, and operating practices.

7. Ask your associates to join you in correcting the organization's short comings.

8. Ask your associates to join you in approaching all those they have harmed, apologize, and make direct amends wherever possible.

9. Continue to take personal inventory, and, when you are wrong, promptly admit it.

10. Seek through ongoing dialogue to improve your consciousness and that of others, and act on what you learn.

11. Carry this message to other parts of the organization, and practice these principles in all of your affairs.

12. Seek commitment to these practices from key people in the organizational change process.

THE LIVING MIRRORS

Arthur and the knights are living mirrors. They reflect each others' virtues and vices, interests and aversions, and—in some measure—the values of the organization as a whole. Looking glasses sometimes distort, however, depending on their size, distance from the object reflected, quality, and the intensity of available light. Living mirrors are harmonically rather than causally linked.

They reflect not each other but, like members of an orchestra, the waves of the conductor's baton and more. Part of the sound we hear comes from the score; part from each musician's training, history, and anticipated future; part from the collaboration and talent of the individual players; and part from the pacing, intensity, emphasis, and skill of the conductor. *In no way, does the conductor create the performance, which results from the interaction of the orchestra members.* The music's beauty depends on the clarity, perfection, and intensity of each person's intent and performance rather than on anyone's position in the orchestra.

In any group, consciousness—and the individual powers of which it is a function—varies. Some people focus almost exclusively on themselves; some, on themselves and a few others. A few individuals' consciousness extends beyond their own interests and surroundings to the system—the organization, community, nation, and planet—as a whole.

My premise is that the impact of one person on others in a corporation is a function of his or her breadth of consciousness. Consciousness underscores true company hierarchies, and the search for Arthur is the search to find an individual who is best able to mirror the entire system. In the first few years of my professional life, I was not able to see the remarkable effects of living mirrors in organizations.

+≕

FROM KNIGHT TO KING

Initially, I worked only for knights who served as middle managers. They often had considerable local influence, but little pull with the top executives. While we did significant work together within their work spheres, we were always hampered by fear of speaking freely to the hierarchy and by unspoken territorial boundaries.

For years, I never really noted these constraints, because we were having such a good time making a difference and helping knights achieve their goals. For a long time, the fact that there were places we could not go escaped me altogether. Even the closed doors were invisible. The top bosses existed only as benign names on offices or letterheads. They didn't seem to interfere and were rarely around.

On the other hand, the knights were my pals. I met their spouses and children and ate in their homes. I counseled their marriages and became partners in their careers. I was only really acquainted with these knights, their technical staffs, and their secretaries. Two strata escaped my scrutiny:

- The workers—people in white overalls someplace else doing something else: I had nothing to sell to them, and they had no money to spend on me, so we never met.
- The top bosses—shadowy people in three-piece suits with corner offices where I did not venture.

During these years, a sense of powerlessness crept up on me. No matter what I or they did, we pretty much stayed on a course we hadn't set. The corporate vehicle kept turning and twisting to someone else's plan; the best we could do was to try to hold the wheel on the road and go along for the ride. In countless meetings, we filled thousands of pages of flip-chart paper. Over time, I noticed that it little mattered what company, government agency, nonprofit organization, or school for which I was working: The sentences on the flip charts were essentially the same. Typically, they pontificated:

- Leadership doesn't communicate.
- Turf interests are more important than substance.
- Efforts to improve change from one month to another.
- Senior management doesn't have the courage to take real risks.
- Workers won't own the company's problems.
- There isn't enough mutual trust or respect to create a real team.

"These countries must have kings somewhere," I thought, after hitting an organization's brick wall once too often. I decided not to work for knights, though I would continue to respect and interact with

75

them. My clients increasingly became the managers of organizations who held control of resources, finances, and policy.

Dealing with Arthur directly, however, brought a whole new set of problems. At first, it was a great relief to work with people who could spend what was necessary and who could make anyone come to a meeting. With this (apparent) access to whole organizations, my role enlarged, became more complex, and seemed to have greater impact.

It wasn't long, however, before I noticed that both Arthur and the knights spent much of their private time talking about each other. Executives were always planning to develop the staff—analyzing who was stuck, who had a promising future, and who didn't. Middle managers gossiped about each other, discussed what they thought might be on the boss' mind, wondered whether there was some chance s/he would leave the company, and explained how their pet project would improve dramatically if only the boss would give it more attention.

Access to the whole organization had only given me a wider view of grand corporate soap operas. Company limitations now seemed to come from *both* Arthur and the knights, individually and as a group. My clients had changed, but the words people wrote on the miles of flip-chart paper remained the same.

My expectation that finding the right executive would provide the keys to a company's kingdom had proved too simple. I was now walking in a world of mirrors.

⊨

REFLECTIONS

The knights mirror Arthur. What's possible for the knights of the Round Table is typically limited by what's possible for Arthur. The knights can usually tell what Arthur will:
- or will not listen to.
- suppress.

- ❧ permit in spite of possible upset in the group.
- ❧ allow in conflict resolution among groups.
- ❧ prefer as important (financial, marketing, research, production, information, relationship, etc.).
- ❧ single out to reframe every problem in its light.

When the last case is true, much of what happens aims to enable or avoid concerns in this special area. And, then, the organization may find itself either usefully—or too narrowly—focused. Spectators at the British game of cricket are described as being "in the terrace." The players or participants in the game are "on the pitch." Arthur's exclamation "I'm for this!" should call for knightly action "on the pitch," as the Round Table follows Arthur's intention. Senior leaders constantly process their experience and activity according to Arthur's personal views. Even though Arthur may not state them explicitly, the knights understand, judging by how Arthur deals with people, with themselves, and with others.

Suppose Arthur will not let the knights work out their problems, especially team problems, in groups—that is, at the Round Table. Either Arthur's knights will then go out to their domains and replicate the scene they had with Arthur, not letting teams in their own areas resolve problems as a group, or the knights will resist or ignore Arthur's example. The net effect in any case is that the entire organization has been influenced by the chief executive officer's intent. Everyone operates within or against Arthur's determined behavior. What happens in the knights' domains is a reflection of—and is limited by—the integrated and unintegrated aspects of Arthur's personal expression.

The knights' values and their ability to express and act upon them tend to mirror Arthur's limits. Among these issues are the knights':
- ❧ ability to abstract.
- ❧ limits on self-expression.
- ❧ emotional range.
- ❧ toleration of different kinds of contact.
- ❧ resolution of differences.

⇢ ability to work as a team.

⇢ breadth of chosen responsibility.

Arthur mirrors the knights: What's possible for them becomes what's possible for him. Knights of the Round Table serve their people as loyally as they do their king. Loyalty, honor, service, and fidelity to the quest were characteristic of the age of chivalry. Nobility was not merely a hereditary class; it was a quality of life.

The Courage to Confront

In corporate America, individual and collective acts of knightly courage are not unknown. Such behaviors can transcend what seem to be unshakable historic limits, and, if Arthur mirrors the knights' courage, the result can be immediate, drastic, meaningful change. I recently witnessed such a dramatic act of Arthurian mirroring as a company's knights, formerly intimidated by a tyrannical boss, created a Round Table out of their own courage and generosity. I saw what my own history predicted could not happen: Subordinates, in the face of arbitrary intelligence and force, through their own initiative and radiance shaped an altogether different reality, a harmony of differing business interests.

This 100-year-old international financial services company, with more than 50,000 employees spread across five continents, operated within the context of its iron traditions and the obdurate, opinionated genius of its chief executive officer. Arthur, who collected expensive paintings, sculpture, tapestries, and furniture, had turned corporate command and control of his company into its own fine art. His acerbic wit and interrogative response to threat transformed perfectly capable men and women into helpless children. He *seemed* the perfect elitist boss, a masterpiece of elegant domination, the king of the put-down, and the lord of the unanswerable question. In private conversation, however, he revealed himself as an unhappy melancholic man, disappointed and frustrated with his senior team, questioning not only his future with the company but also the meaning of his own life.

By chance, Arthur was called away during one of our scheduled sessions. The knights' conversation turned immediately to the problem their leader represented. After a while, however, his culpability became less clear, as some argued that the problem was their own lack of honesty and courage. Others pointed to the chief executive's genius and contribution to each of them and to the company.

The knights' perceptions of themselves and their leader became more distinct. Their commitment to direct speaking and personal freedom, coupled with their sincere, if ambivalent, appreciation for Arthur made them rise above their normally intimidated state to become more perfect *in terms of their own values*. As living mirrors, the knights' new level of perceptive clarity and adherence to their values led them to take active part in the creation of the Round Table.

After three hours of open discussion, the knights concluded that, the next morning, they would tell Arthur the truth about his negative personal effect on performance and, sincerely and generously, affirm his magnificent gifts to the company and contributions to their individual achievements. The evening ended in a mood of both enthusiasm and fear.

The next morning, with the skillful guidance of one of the senior team members, the knights told the truth. For about an hour, a Round Table met, and the multinational company had a new future. Knights and the king proposed and discussed new products and processes. We were all working in the presence of a single aligned intelligence, and anything seemed possible.

As I sat in the morning meeting, participants spoke as into mirrors—not to themselves but to images of others, who also mirrored, spoke, and listened. In this odd and splendid moment, the king had become a vulnerable, appreciative man in dialogue with people willing to risk their positions by honestly expressing both admiration and displeasure. Each person seemed to be a living mirror, with his or her unique point of view and internal script. A communicative Round Table had emerged from the ashes of a frightened, suppressed, careful gathering dominated by an upset, arrogant leader.

The Table Splinters

Unfortunately, this Round Table collapsed the same day it created itself. Unable to bear his vulnerability, Arthur was quick to reassert himself. His self-centered genius filled the room and trampled the short-lived Round Table. For a moment, the room had glittered with living mirrors, but the burst of equality shattered, as Arthur's defense mechanisms and automatic response to what he perceived as threat emerged triumphant. Without conscious, self-managed maintenance techniques, Camelot is always short-lived.

Hierarchy can also distort the reflections in the living mirrors. Among the findings in Barry Oshry's remarkable body of research (see particularly 1977), only a few people at the top of an organizational system have what he calls "director power." From that position, they control the organization's most valued resources: its rewards, careers, fundamental directions. According to Oshry, only the person with director power can create or eliminate organization structures. The middle-level mangers—knights—Oshry says, control the flow of information in an organization. They do not create organizational structure nor control work itself. Only the workers control work, and their true influence on the system rests in their ability to participate whole heartedly or to rebel.

One's ability to reflect reality in the living mirrors can be distorted by the point of view inherent in the power of one's position. A system's reality itself is shaped by its top executives, middle managers, and workers. To be able to see all three layers in play is a rare gift that develops only through sustained practice.

+=

ARTHUR'S ESSENTIAL ENERGIES

I have attended the last three annual general managers' meetings of EMCO, a combined $800-million distribution and $300-million building products manufacturing company based in Ontario. At first, interdivisional conflict seethed just below the surface, staff approached cross-functional projects with suspicion, the mood was cautious, and most new ideas were received critically. Some of this uncertainty could have been attributed to a recession and job losses from downsizing. But, whatever the cause, the company formed no Round Table.

In the third year, the atmosphere among members of the same group was wide open. People spoke out clearly and vulnerably about what was missing and what was stuck. Cross-divisional project presentations were buoyant and crisp and were presented in a spirit of partnership.

Why? Through quality awareness programs, almost all managers and staff had come to realize that what they did personally had an enormous impact on the quality of the company. The Merlin process and a management-wide exercise in partnering had allowed a new level of trust to develop.

As the most recent three-day meeting progressed, Frank M. Hennessey, EMCO's president and chief executive officer, made certain that his 70 general managers sustained positive energy by providing the kind of energy missing but necessary at any point in time. In response, there was a simultaneous experience of a Round Table—an inspired group of men and women whose intelligence and energies were aligned toward creating a single entity, a partnership among themselves.

<hr>

ARTHURIAN QUALITIES

Persistence

The Round Table is under constant assault. Disgruntled knights, contenders for the throne, customer problems, and economic recessions combine with everyday entropy to deform it. Arthur, therefore, constantly needs to speak out for the Round Table and its strategic intent. The quality relationships that make up a Round Table persist only when people infuse energy into them.

At one point in this latest general managers' meeting, Hennessey referred to a statement he made three years earlier that "We will change the culture of this company." He and his listeners were sure that a radical change in context was coming then, and they were right. Where there is will and persistence, doubt disappears, replaced by demand. Perhaps the mind can deal only with persistence or doubt at one time. With a shared vision like that developed by Hennessey's general managers, Arthur's constant demanding call to arms seems neither suppressive nor manipulative. Instead, it offers an enlivening channel for the release and focus of energies.

Safety

Part of Arthur's charge is to provide a safe haven. In safety, people's enhanced energy for a Round Table flows freely; they are cooperative and open; they work in a spirit of partnership and collegiality. In an insecure environment, only command and control can assure cooperation, and the possibility of capturing people's hearts as well as their minds diminishes.

The EMCO general managers meeting was safe for participants because Hennessey made it so. He guaranteed safety by talking repeatedly of his commitment to individual and collective success, citing examples of people contributing to each other's accomplishments, inviting dialogue, and checking back to assure its quality. He consistently emphasized how difficult openness is in a hierarchy without interpersonal commitment and responded honestly and appropriately. He chose to be responsible for people's safety because, as their colleague in the Round Table, he saw maintaining their comfort as part of his job.

Later, Hennessey admitted that he'd had "to learn a lot about making situations safe for people." He speculated that, although perhaps his patience and commitment to people's success contributed to their comfort, the same qualities "sometimes got in the way of my making necessary demands for speed and asking them to strive for excellence rather than be content with mediocre performance."

He continued,

> Finally, I was faced with a situation where I wasn't holding a key person accountable to standards to which he and I had previously agreed. The price of my protecting him and making him feel safe was that his career was in jeopardy.
>
> Not until I deeply and seriously challenged his capabilities and management methods did he feel a desire to change. The result? Thanks to the changes he made, his division is now doing brilliantly. He is, in fact, safer now that he was before!
>
> It's a paradox. Safety, which is critical, relates to both empowerment and responsibility and depends on particular boss-subordinate relationships. It also depends on personal views of the truth.

Creating a safe corporate environment, he concluded, does not always mean being gentle and protective.

Authentic Presence

Also part of Arthur's charge is to be authentic. Carl R. Rogers (1961) defined authenticity as congruence between one's thoughts, feelings, and actions. Authentic presence, while hard to define, is also often hard to access because it can be clouded by concerns, opinions, and certainties. Some people make an impression; others don't. At parties, some people stand out; others are quickly forgotten. Some people insist that they trust you, but, somehow, you don't believe them. It's just not there the way the rain is there when it falls on your face. Some people say they are committed to the team, but no one senses their authentic presence on it.

Children at play have authentic presence: They have no hidden agenda. What you see is what you get. They are emotionally and spiritually at home, and their clear eyes warm to you as do you to them. We can learn from them: Presence comes from authenticity, from being true to oneself, and from being open and honest about one's experience, no matter what.

Authenticity and presence are both Glastonbury and Avalon phenomena. In front of a medieval castle in Germany—on the surface, all severe Glastonbury: white paint, windows, flowers, cobblestones, metal grates, and towers—suddenly, I found myself in the breathtaking presence of Avalon as well. The building I had seen a moment before had been touched by the hand of magic; the spirit there in its creation was still present.

Such presence is hard to explain, but instantly recognizable. Some people have it, some don't. When Arthur is authentic and present, vast energies flow in an organization. The distortion of boss-subordinate relations dissolves momentarily, and the opportunity for authenticity opens among all the players. In 1785, Thomas Jefferson wrote that "commerce between master and servant is despotism." In companies, rigid hierarchies can be a problem waiting to happen that can inhibit the development of a Round Table. At the EMCO general managers' meeting, Hennessey was utterly himself, and others responded by being utterly themselves. The energy and excitement present seemed to make the future more a gateway than a wall.

The more authentic the presence Arthur brings to employees, the more is vision possible. The more vision is believed, the more energy is released into the system. Likewise, vision fades as presence recedes: The more Arthur is seen as remote, manipulative, controlling, and emotionally unavailable, the less true seem statements of vision. The Arthurian imperative does not seek a Round Table for the sake of itself. It is always in service of the organization's equivalent of the Holy Grail—strategic intent and shared vision.

According to Russian philosopher, Nicholas Berdayev, "Only a prophetic vision of the past can set history in motion; and only a prophetic vision of the future can bind the present and the past into a sort of interior and complete spiritual movement . . ." (quoted in Tolstoy, 1988, p. xix). If, as is all too often the case, a company vision is contrived only to solve an immediate problem or is offered as a shallow compromise among people unwilling to conflict openly, the magic is missing. It's difficult for business people to talk about visionary or spiritual experiences in corporate contexts. Executives typically couch what they say in safe terms—financial or other.

But the reality is that when people are trying to build something great, something world class, they have to believe it, live it, talk it into existence, and *not be afraid of looking silly*. Capturing hearts as well as minds means uplifting spirits.

And that means finding and expressing what will uplift one's own.

Unconditional Caring

We all learn to give up the childlike trust and openness that once accepted our parents' undemanding love. When I meet a stranger who seems to care for me without apparent reason, I become at least suspicious and often withdrawn. While I truly want to be admired, I often distrust its actual occurrence, except when the caring comes from my family or a few trusted others. No wonder organizations are wary, cautious places.

While almost everyone wants to be cared for, we swim in an ocean of resistance and caution. To create a Round Table in the face of this fear takes the Arthurian leadership that can release the immense energy available. Arthur's task is to care unconditionally for Round Table candidates.

One chief executive officer admitted to me that he would never have the strength to commit to an illogical possibility without the support of an aligned group of colleagues. To fulfill his quest to make his company the "best pharmaceutical company of its kind in North

America," he had to create a Round Table. Tacit, lukewarm, covert support from his knights—those persons he had chosen and who had promised to take the risk with him—was not enough.

The opposition of people in peripheral jobs is often unimportant. From others, however, anything less than full participation is unacceptable. Without such commitment, Arthur will face sabotage that could derail both him and his strategic intent. Such people must have a direct, clear choice to engage the challenges of the Round Table fully and personally—or to leave. Only from a vulnerable position can Arthur summon the power from Avalon to provide these options. He must rise above personal anger to win this harmony.

Possibility

Boundless possibility and limitless energy go together. Without the uniquely human phenomenon of a sense of possibility, boredom, hopelessness, and stuckness can follow. Arthur's ability to generate a sense of possibility with and for others is an essential hallmark of his reign.

A sense of possibility, as fragile and easily squashed as a guppy or a gerbil, is maintained by conscious speaking and deliberate generation. Part of Arthur's challenge, therefore, is to keep a conversation for possibility alive in the organization at all times. In 1958, Winston Churchill wrote that George Marshall "always fought victoriously over defeatism, discouragement, and disillusion"; true, and so do successful leaders like Frank Hennessey, who consistently devote themselves to the creation of a sense of possibility, which:
- frees the human spirit.
- creates willingness to trust and cooperate where it previously didn't exist.
- allows rich speculation between people that often results in new ideas and ways of thinking.

Whether as cheerleader, coach, orator, boss, friend, or partner, Arthur keeps possibility alive by personal example and by assuring that business conversations aim at and return to feasible accomplishments. Those who live in the realm of the possible steer clear of paralysis.

Inquiry

To inquire is to:

- ask a question and not base what you hear on what you already think you know.
- seek new knowledge and be open to surprise.
- explore and delight in what is uncertain.
- attend to your confusion moment-by-moment rather than adhere rigidly to your certainty.
- ask questions with a commitment to the further questions revealed in the response, rather than a commitment to finding the right answer.

Essential as it should be, inquiry is rare in organizations. Most people don't risk it, instead steering conversations toward intended outcomes, because they fear that an open process may produce a negative result. Affirming the spirit of inquiry does not ask that executives relinquish their values or their principles. It does mean, however, that they *participate* in the process of change, not simply *direct* it.

To sustain the spirit of inquiry takes discipline and skill, but it offers tremendous potential rewards: Inquiry can release the energy necessary to build a Round Table in any size group. It works as well with 300 people as with 6. True inquiry neither forbids responses nor manipulates or forces. Cooperation is a de facto accompaniment of the process.

Suppression, the enemy to building a Round Table, is the opposite of inquiry, which is an expression of personal freedom. Free inquiry:

- releases participants from the command and control paradigm that pervades hierarchical organizations and their leaders.
- captures minds and hearts because it creates a possibility of pure choice about the subject at hand.
- gives people choice not based on incentives, arguments or threats.

When Arthur inquires himself and faithfully sustains the spirit of inquiry in others, the invisible Round Table emerges into the light.

Values

Arthur operates from fundamental values, rooted in optimism and caring, which are worth any sacrifice, not merely from interests, based in survival. One person's fundamental value *could* be another's interest. Values, however, carry with them a sense of nobility and contribution; interests focus on protection or aggrandizement. Hennessey's ability to harness the right energy at the right time, while calling consistently on his values, suggests that such a basis of action can activate impressive amounts of otherwise dormant energy.

The great Jewish philosopher Abraham Joshua Heschel (1955) calls interests the value-blind man's Seeing Eye dog. The prevalence of interest-based behavior in business is one reason many organizations have trouble changing. Joining earth and space was for Barthelemy essential, however, not merely in his interest. (See page 62.) Similarly, when John Kennedy invited us to "Ask not what your country can do for you; ask what you can do for your country," he expressed the fundamental value of people contributing to one another and released vast energy in the nation, for a time, making most Americans feel proud and united. When Mohandas Gandhi challenged India to expel the British and claim the freedom that was for him a fundamental value, the nation was transformed, as widespread energy generated a political and social revolution. Similarly, when business leaders speak from fundamental values, they may uncover enormous productive energy, even in the face of failure and on plateaus of uninspired performance.

As Serge Kahili King believes, power comes from within, and its source is in fundamental values (1990). It's rare that the courage to speak as did a Kennedy or a Gandhi appears in the business world. The danger of appearing foolish or dreamy seems so real and the need to survive so paramount that leaders' deeply held values are often muffled in the face of politics, competition, economics, and desire for dignity in a world where the social reality is that short-term numbers are what really count. Business seems unable to fulfill fundamental values, even though they are sometimes articulated and published. And fundamental values merely expressed are experienced as momentarily uplifting instruments, not as overriding present intentions. Without real commitment, leaders cannot sustain and release even their own energy— much less anyone else's—in a day-to-day, interest-driven reality.

For example, there's lots of current talk about the need to be customer focused and customer driven, but few such businesses actually are operating. The value-based shift in thinking that would allow an overriding commitment to customers' prosperity is beyond what most establishments are willing to conceive or risk.

Nonetheless, value-driven businesses are feasible and are increasingly in evidence. Mary Scott and Howard Rothman describe 12 companies "with a conscience" (1992). The truism that the purpose of business is business means that it focuses is on making money. But a question remains: Should profit be the initial generating purpose or should it be a required measure of success? Either answer can be paramount. Whichever is, creates the world for those involved in the company.

The Body Shop, a value-driven business, is a rapidly expanding, financially successful international retailer of "cruelty-free" soaps, lotions, and cosmetics. In 1995, The Body Shop had 1,210 branches in 45 countries, trading in 23 languages. On average, a new branch opens every two and a half days. It sold £500.1 million ($803.7 million) worth of products (up 16 percent from the year before), running up a pretax profit of £33.5 million ($53.8 million, up 17 percent).

The Body Shop prides itself not only on its refusal to harm animals to test its products but also its humane treatment of its employees and its commitment to programs designed to achieve social justice such as "Trade not Aid." The latter encourages business enterprises for the disadvantaged and homeless both at home and abroad. Excerpts from the Body Shop's "Trading Charter" proclaim,

The way we trade creates profits with principles. . . .

We aim to ensure that human and civil rights, as set out in the Universal Declaration of Human Rights, are respected throughout our business activities. . . .

We . . . support long-term, sustainable relationships with communities in need . . . [paying] special attention to minority groups, women, and disadvantaged peoples . . . .

We . . . use environmentally sustainable resources wherever technically and economically viable. . . .

We . . . promote animal protection throughout our business activities. . . .

We . . . institute appropriate monitoring, auditing, and disclosure mechanisms to ensure our accountability and demonstrate our compliance with these principles. (The Body Shop, 1995, p. 14)

Body Shop Founder and Chief Executive Officer Anita Roddick, described in company publicity as "a rebel *with* a cause . . . shaped by the forces of the 1950s and 1960s (everything from James Dean and protest marches to backpacking around the world in the days you could still afford to)," summarizes her company's philosophy in a 1994 brochure as follows:

Business shapes the world. It is capable of changing the world almost any way you can imagine. The decisions of business people affect the lives and well-being of millions of people. So, God help us if those decisions aren't guided by a moral code of behavior. I can't wait for the day when we replace the value of money with a different set of values, like the value of nature leading to sustainability, value for people based on fulfillment and social justice, and value for human relationships through friendship. (1994, p. 1)

Practice

To be Arthur means to be able to see when energy is missing and provide it. As a goal, this activity can be tedious and burdensome. As dedicated practice, it can be a lifelong source of energy and an example to others.

Mastering both Glastonbury and Avalon values will produce corporate alignment and business results. Each of us tends to see and favor one or the other mindset, however; thus, only lifelong practice integrates them seamlessly. If successful, Arthur learns to love this practice, which can become the guiding force for revitalizing a company. Practice separates Arthur from pretenders. Even the legendary king, however, could not attain perfection.

George Leonard (1991) notes three typical types of individuals who aspire to corporate development: dabblers, hackers, and obsessives.

- Dabblers approach each new project, opportunity, or job with enormous enthusiasm. They revel in its newness and talk about it endlessly—so long as the glow is on—but, when they reach the first plateau, their enthusiasm wanes rapidly. The dabbler will return to the activity periodically, but without conviction.
- Hackers also start out enthusiastically, but they do not practice. After getting the basic idea, they stick with the project but are willing to stay on the plateau indefinitely.
- Obsessives believe only in results. They want to be the best early in the game, so when they reach the first plateau, their annoyance at the absence of immediate results makes them redouble their efforts. If this spurt doesn't produce a breakthrough, they seek another game.

Leonard believes that "mastery" (the title of his book) comes from learning to love the plateau: When the practice itself becomes what is valued, then the game is endless and improvement will be continuous. Pleasure no longer comes merely from the achievement but from the journey. The corporate leaders I know who are, in fact, most accomplished and satisfied, are those who most practice their chosen discipline. The transformation from being goal-oriented to being practice-oriented is the first step on the path to becoming Arthur.

⊨

ENERGY COMES FROM AVALON

Energy, an Avalon phenomenon, is often shrouded in mists and therefore cannot be seen directly, but it is there. Sometimes energy is intellectual, manifesting itself in great ideas, active intelligence, critical thinking, and brilliant abstractions. Sometimes it is emotional and spiritual, appearing as joy, sadness, or anger. At other times, it is physical, showing itself as the tension or relaxation in people's physical movements.

An organization is an energy field in constant vibration. The more Arthur has direct access to this field, the greater is his ability to align people working together successfully in common cause. Over 25 years, I've observed a great many leaders succeed—and fail—to release the human energies needed to build and sustain a corporate Round Table. While many, many energies exist, the eight primary Arthurian behaviors described on pages 81-91 assure a Round Table. Since these energies are constantly drained when people feel threatened, providing missing energies and anticipating their loss is an unending task.

Although people experiencing insufficient energy often try to draw it from others for their personal use, this ploy usually fails for the would-be pirates. Those being robbed, however, often find themselves with lowered energy—even though their loss does not seem to benefit the parasites who would live off them (James Redfield, 1994).

4 THE QUESTING BEAST
Principles for a Round Table

The Questing Beast has the head of a serpent, the body of a leop-ard, the buttocks of a lion, and the feet of a hart. From its belly issues the sound of 30 yapping hounds. It is never brought to earth.

—Sir Thomas Malory (1485/1978)

 n response to attempts to change it, a culture becomes a questing beast. But creating a corporate Round Table almost always demands drastic, far-reaching change to the business-as-usual status quo.

Kurt Lewin, one of the founders of 20th-century behav-ioral science, once said that the best way to understand anything is to try to change it (1951). For 26 years, I've worked with leaders to change their organizations' cultures and processes. Unfortunately, what most stands out in memory are the times when the executives themselves derailed positive cultural growth. Their roadblocks, never malicious, were justified for sensible reasons, including:

- excess cost.
- too little time.
- insufficient political support.
- potentially disagreeable prospects or process.
- the need to spend time with customers.
- flagging personal energy.
- competing priorities.
- remission of the original pain that prompted the request for help.

Out of a long history of both success and failure have evolved certain principles on how fundamentally to change a company. They will make many executives as uncomfortable as they do me: Chaos is disturbing enough, but the false expectation of order is worse. Both in retrospect and in planning stages, culture change processes seem linear, even sequential. The journey appears to unfold logically, from planning and design meetings, to workshops and intensive educational programs, all aspects cemented in ongoing, real-time management and the building of partnerships.

And Phase I *does* typically consist of seeking strategic visions, developing teams, setting stretch goals (pages 103–107), and planning for the desired culture change. Phase II *does* often involve enlisting widespread support and commitment, addressing intractable problems, and finding personal limits regarding action and results. Phase III *does* usually consist of reengineering processes and developing champions of, and ongoing constituencies for, change.

In any moment of execution, however, culture change processes may suddenly encounter unexpected existing political, social, technical, and personal obstacles. Those who try to hold to a linear process will be distracted from what is real in the moment. Focus on plan can suppress consciousness, and magic comes from the latter.

Each principle for culture change can be contained in any of the others. The same process never works quite the same way twice.

What really matters is how effectively one deals with what's missing, what's stuck, what's working, and what's possible *now*. What really matters is doing instead of talking. The principles elaborated in this chapter can help leaders succeed in achieving culture change—rather than stopping it before it begins or aborting it in its early stages.

―⇌―

ENSHRINE TRUTH

—TELL THE WHOLE TRUTH TO THE KEY PEOPLE ALL THE TIME

Key people—whoever Arthur needs to make critical changes happen—may reside anywhere in an organization. They must, however, be champions of change committed to the corporation's collective values and aspirations. Anything left unsaid or withheld in a relationship becomes the boundary of future possibility and action in all mutually affected interactions. The affair that Lancelot and Guinevere concealed from Arthur eventually poisoned the air of the whole kingdom with an unshared secret. A company is in some ways like a marriage; it shrivels when substance or intensity is withheld.

For example, one company chair did not tell her vice president that his inability to support her basic values and her commitment to culture change meant that he would never become chief executive officer. Sometimes the chair sidled up to this problem, dropped hints about it, or cited parallel examples, but she never was completely frank. Her failure to be honest with her vice president eventually halted her hoped-for culture change because—innocently or by design— he led his division down a separate path that undermined her grand intentions for the company.

What could have been contagious company-wide change dwindled. The chair's noble vision failed because she lacked the courage to tell a key player the whole truth. Maintaining a political distance from people who are unessential allies for change may sometimes be expedient; however, even this compromise may have destructive consequences. Culture change, like team spirit, is vital, transparent, ephemeral, and easily dashed.

―

RECOGNIZE THAT THE SWORD IS STILL IN THE STONE

—ADMIT THAT THE WAY THE COMPANY IS OPERATING WILL NOT ACHIEVE THE DESIRED FUTURE, AND ACKNOWLEDGE WHERE IT IS STUCK

Owning up to the fact that an organization is on the wrong track is not easy. Arthur and the knights usually prefer to equivocate:

- We have a problem, but we are already working on it.
- This situation really isn't a problem. It's more of an opportunity.
- The difficulty is one of a number of challenges we face.
- There is nothing *fundamentally* wrong here; there are just some minor problems to fix.
- If we had more time and better resources, we could handle the situation.

None of these statements admits stuckness and the failure of past attempts to solve what's wrong. Almost everyone is deeply attached— sometimes addicted—to the status quo, and most people go to great lengths to avoid acknowledging that they do not have control over something about which they care so much as the basic ways their companies operate. Members of senior leadership teams often need to look good to one another and to themselves and to protect their power base by justifying past actions.

Such teams may genuinely be trying to address fundamental problems in an apparently solid, analytic fashion. In attempting to resolve their companies' cultural problems conceptually, they may conceive a brilliant vision, develop a solid strategic plan based on a statement of core values, and disseminate it widely. But almost nothing changes, because they never transcend their attachments to the past and the present.

In Arthurian legend, Gawain must confess his betrayal before the Green Knight will accept him. In the corporate sphere, without full recognition and admission of the failure of present methods and results, subsequent activities will be incremental, rooted in prior culture, and ineffective.

CREATE KNIGHTS, PLEDGE THEIR FUTURE

—COMMIT TO INDIVIDUALS' DEVELOPMENT AND THEIR SUCCESS

Culture lives in people's minds: When people don't constantly (if slowly) become more conscious, skilled, and talented in ways that serve the future, the organization is constrained by existing core competencies and limitations. If key people don't develop, culture change is impossible.

Although many fine systems of performance appraisal and coaching are available, most of them only find limited or temporary use. Why? I think because the underlying truth is that most leaders prefer to use the known talents of key people to fulfill business priorities rather than to engage with the messy, unpredictable, long-term experience of growth. Some executives are willing to help their staff develop, but their basis for action, however commendable, often remains unclear.

For example, certain respected centers of academic excellence accept only bright, aggressive careerists-to-be, who are almost sure to do well later, no matter what they do or don't learn. To assure vibrant talent and energies among their new employees, some companies hire exclusively graduates of these prescreened talent pools. The superb staffs such policies recruit may offer companies a certain latitude not to hurry in implementing career development opportunities early; however, their new employees' excellence often results more from smart selection than intentional corporate development. I know of one public accounting firm that hires top students and, after five years, retains 17 percent of them. The firm has a rigorous accultura-tion system, requiring long hours and close apprenticeships. People receive frequent, clear feedback on how they are doing, measured by explicit, forward-looking criteria. It appears that the people who develop through these procedures survive, stay the course, and even-tually become partners. It may also be true, however, that those who remain are the ones who are willing to embrace the rigor. In this case, the process may have less to do with development than with dese-lecting those who won't claim the culture as their own.

On good days, I believe people can be developed intentionally. On bad days, the same problems seem to come up over and over, and the hope that someone will develop feels like an incomplete sentence or a joke without a punch line. People development is a subject I wish would go away. I once heard it compared to farming: You spade up the patch, plant seeds, weed the garden, water the field, fertilize as need-ed, and, sure enough, some of the seeds will sprout. But don't bet on which seeds will grow and which won't.

For most of my life I had little interest in developing anybody except myself and none in being developed by anyone else. I figured that if people were talented, I would relate to them in terms of their excellence; if they weren't, they could go elsewhere. Nobody had ever done much to develop me, and "conscious development" efforts seemed only an opportunity to sell training programs.

This system worked reasonably well, so long as I didn't need any-thing but occasional help. Then everything changed. My company wouldn't grow unless its culture changed, and its culture wouldn't change unless people developed. I could no longer just pray for rain on the garden or find part-time farmers to fill in. For the first time in my life, I took people development seriously. The result was that a lot of people did develop in the desired direction *so long as I was committed to them and willing to spend the necessary time with them.* The process is messy; it requires specific standards and feedback; it is unpredictable; and it doesn't follow a timetable. In retrospect, it's well worth the trouble, but, like so much else, I only learned its value when I had to. The good news is that the emerging culture contains a remarkable future for both clients and colleagues, a future calling for teamwork and mutual support.

I don't know what the world would look like if all people had others truly committed to their development. I suspect that organizational structure, hierarchies, growth, and relationships would all look different and, probably, would be improved. Maybe such a cooperative situation is impossible in companies as currently constituted. Still, only through commitment-based people development can a company's future fulfill the powers of the imagination and not simply the possibilities of the past.

+═

SEEK MERLIN

—FOLLOW YOUR PARTNER'S ADVICE

Writer Rita M. Brown defined insanity as "doing the same thing over and over and expecting a different result." Four-thousand calorie days make people fat whether they eat sitting down, standing up, or in the dark. Not saving money leads to poverty, no matter how much fun spending it is. Ignoring customers' wishes makes a company's future a struggle.

Changing a company's culture requires independent help—often, although not always, from outside. A company's internal approach, influenced by the existing culture of agreements, concerns, values, and perceptions, inevitably shapes (and often limits) corporate thinking. An innocent eye, unprogrammed by expectations, offers a new place to stand and a new point of view. Only pure Percival can glimpse the Grail.

Without partnership, most organizations can't get there from here. Merlin must be trusted to point out what's missing in a company's

Glastonbury and its Avalon. Typically, a partner is a consultant or colleague with a record of helping people change their corporate cultures. Many leaders, however, resist advice from peers and subordinates hardest in the areas where the company is most stubbornly stuck. For this very reason, such partnership often has to come from outside.

—

FIND THE HORIZON, *THEN* SCALE THE BATTLEMENTS

—IDENTIFY PERSONAL BELIEFS THAT LIMIT ACHIEVEMENT

Sometimes it happens that I awaken at night and start to worry about some great difficulty. I decide that I must speak to the Pope about it. Then I awaken more fully and remember that I am the Pope.

—Pope John XXIII[13]

Without Arthur and the knights' creation of moments of real choice, history—good and bad—will repeat itself. Leaders will fail to communicate. Repetitive, unproductive activities will continue, and disempowering attachments will flourish. Glastonbury will continue to dominate Avalon or vice versa. And leaders will not ask for help from partners and coaches.

Explanations are double-edged swords, both describing what happens and limiting future action. A fundamental assumption associated with something a senior leader fears becomes an all-powerful, self-limiting paradigm, a transparent box in which the entire company has to operate. But those boxes can dissolve.

The director of development of a multinational advertising agency, dissatisfied by slow introductions of clients to products, was originally afraid to ask for an obviously necessary increase in speed. His reluc-

---

[13]As quoted in Bodian (1993, p. 56)

tance was understandable: If what he really wanted happened, he would have to do a lot more of what he didn't want to do. And his schedule, already hopelessly overbooked, would be subject to increased demands. Finally, he loved his vision of himself as "Mr. Nice Guy." To make his company work the way it should, he would have to ask lackadaisical employees to shape up, and he would probably have to require some overtime. Was efficiency worth his subordinates' anger? he pondered.

When he was able to recognize his entrapment in an achievement-limiting belief, however, he invented a new paradigm for new product introduction. From then on, he began asking for what he wanted and dealt with the consequences as they occurred. The clients finally got the results they wanted; the staff—while they grumbled initially—became proud of their effective performance; and the director freed himself of his own mental tyranny.

Achievement-limiting personal beliefs can paralyze company cultures. Every time a fear-based explanation for failure is banished, people find freedom, make effective choices, and produce dramatic progress.

Every huge leap forward in performance comes when people change what they believe. For example, several years ago in northern England, after years of minor, incremental change, factory workers stopped believing their training manuals, transcended their self-doubts, and doubled machine efficiencies. Their progress is an excellent example of how Jinny S. Ditzler's 10-step process for setting—and reaching—goals that transcend achievement-limited beliefs can work (1994).

BELIEVE IN CAMELOT

—INVENT AN ATTRACTIVE, UNTHINKABLE FUTURE

Culture—the structure of interpretation that organizes reality—is pervasive. It tells people what is tabu, what is possible, what can be said, what cannot be said, and, ultimately, even what can be thought. Culture change, therefore, demands a new structure of interpretation, a new basis for operating. This requires what is unthinkable in the present, and thinking the unthinkable—a tongue twister—is easier said than done.

The first time I thought the unthinkable, I opened the door to opportunity. While looking for a house to buy, I got lost and mistakenly went into a beautiful home in the woods that cost three times what I could afford. I listened to the realtor's price calmly, went back to my apartment, drank three martinis, ate two large bags of Doritos™, and fell asleep. When I awoke, I was unsettled. I now had a vision of an unthinkable, attractive future. Nonetheless, I *was* considering it, and, after about two years, I *did* buy a similar house.

The stunning achievement of the United Parcel Service offers a corporate example of my stumbling into an unaffordable house—except that their step toward an unrealistic expectation was deliberate. In the early 1940s, the United Parcel Service decided to go into the common carrier business and to compete directly with the U.S. Parcel Post System. The government, which had no monopoly on parcel post, had seen competition before but had always triumphed. It moved almost one billion packages a year in the 1960s, compared to the United Parcel Service volume of some 250 million. Within 20 years, this picture was virtually reversed.

Experiencing the possibility of an unthinkable attractive future, wanting it, and intending it in the face of all discouraging present circumstances, including one's own discomfort, forces companies to think new thoughts. People can wait to fall into an attractive future. Or they can create a future that calls intentionally.

Existing cultures support the status quo, however. Those who try to change or resist the culture have difficulties and often find themselves squeezed back into the mold, either by others or by their own concern about standing out. Often, the staunchest defenders of a culture, even when minimally competent, become its leaders. Mavericks who don't go along with the crowd or culture may make creative contributions, but they will rarely be in control of organizations' most important resources.

Irish writer Frank O'Connor recalls how, as a boy, he and his friends made their way across the countryside until they came to an orchard wall that seemed insurmountably high. At this point, they took off their hats and tossed them over the wall, where they had no choice but to follow them. In the same way, culture change happens when leaders throw their companies' hats over the wall and, along with their staffs, climb up and over after them.

+===

REACH FOR THE STARS, AND STAY ON THE GROUND

—INSTITUTIONALIZE STRETCH AND BE REALISTIC

Life, like a rubber band, can lose its resilience. Stretch, which is always uncharacteristic, comes in many forms: It is:
- a novel idea.
- a significant goal.
- a new, exciting relationship.
- an adventurous sport, activity, or project.
- a new means of organizing.
- an alternative management philosophy.
- an imaginative method of dealing with problems.
- a commitment to accomplish an unfamiliar task.
- a meeting with people whose values differ from yours.
- a working process from a source outside.
- an unsought challenge.

When the Band Petrifies

The citizens in a small midwestern town I once visited have highly developed antennae for detecting anything uncharacteristic. If something new is introduced by accident on TV or by a visitor, it is first ignored, then discouraged, then disparaged, then attacked. Once identified, the offending phenomenon is dispatched. Nothing unexpected ever happens to these good townspeople, who love their neighbors, contribute to society, and work hard. They have no use for stretch.

Many companies also follow this pattern. Most people I know experience stretch only when they are inspired or when they are forced. They revert to stasis as soon as they can. For example, a company for which I once worked intended to engage the techniques of total quality management. When alerted as to the extent of the changes they would have to make, the staff were alarmed and, without knowing it, decided to solve the problem by *saying* the company was following total quality management's principles while actually *doing* business as usual. The "reform" was a joke, of course, but they didn't get it.

They had simply, unwittingly, renamed everything they were doing.

Years ago, I had a client who, most of the time, paid me not to show up. He *said* he liked my ideas; he *said* he liked the impact I had on him and his group; but he had little inclination to actually *work* with me. On several occasions, I flew to meet with him, only to arrive and discover that he wasn't there. For a while, I thought his irresponsibility was giving me a perfect way to make a living. I could simply sit at home, wait for him to call me up and apologize for not keeping an appointment, and arrange to collect his check. Our nonmeetings run down didn't go on for almost two years before I recognized the pattern and, feeling guilty about taking money without accomplishing anything for him, stopped scheduling appointments altogether. Like many corporate leaders, this successful, intelligent gentleman, responsible for the work lives of thousands of people, affirmed the value of stretch goals and bold ventures. But like most of us, he wasn't willing to tolerate the uncertainty and discomfort stretch can bring.

On the one hand, our *heroes and heroines* are brave, resourceful, and ready to reach beyond their grasp: They fly to the moon, win wars, free slaves, give everything up for love, and so on. On the other hand, *we—as real human beings*—often destroy the elasticity that could let us grow.

Stretch-avoidance techniques are easy to identify:
- Commit and then quietly procrastinate.
- Talk it to death.
- Delegate the job to somebody who never produces results.
- Make stretch deadlines and ignore them.
- Don't apply stretch goals and actions to anything vitally important.
- Decide the goal didn't have to be a stretch in the first place.
- Put off dealing with a problem until tomorrow.

Stretching Without Breaking

Without stretch goals, uncharacteristic behavior, and a plan for quick restarts, the old culture sets the limits for performance, attitude, and behavior. The challenge is to find what both creates stretch and maintains respect for individuals. Stretch isn't sacred, but it is intoxicating and addictive, often bringing people and organizations to the edge of the unknown. The fear can be exciting, and shared challenge usually inspires passion and brings the best out of people; however, institutionalizing stretch has its dangers.

Unless broken or decayed, a relaxed rubber band returns to its original size. If stretched too tight for too long, however, it loses its elasticity, grows limp or brittle, and can snap. People are in some ways analogous to rubber bands. For example, one company that tried to institutionalize stretch as a way of life self-induced crises daily. To drive performance, people yelled at each other. Any behavior that did not stretch was ridiculed, shunned, or both. Executives often piled stretch goals on top of one another, and commitment to them was elevated to a cultural norm. When people seemed uncommitted, they were criticized and helped to see their error. Leaders and peers had full permission to counsel others, in the name of the day's stretch goals. Often their advice was delivered abusively. The recipients of this unwanted help often went emotionally underground and left the organization with increasing frequency. Stretch gone mad?

Erving Polster once captured my attention with the statement that "self-improvement is to life as logic is to philosophy—trivial" (personal communication, 1969). I've come to see stretch in much the same way. In order to produce wide-reaching culture change and expected extraordinary performance, stretch commitments and uncharacteristic behavior are essential. Stretch promotes self-renewal and organizational aliveness. Commitment to stretch as a way of life, however, is another tyranny in the face of paradox. Any process that dilutes people's aliveness and possibility—whether aimed at institutionalizing stretch or at guaranteeing predictable, incremental progress—violates Avalon.

We should simultaneously dream the impossible dream and keep our feet firmly on the ground; that is, we should live simultaneously both in Glastonbury and Avalon. In other terms, according to a Zen saying, "After ecstasy comes the laundry." Arthur must seek the Grail, but he must also tend to the needs of the kingdom, and these include collecting taxes, building roads, and caring for the poor.

A fine application of this principle occurred when managers of a retail chain deliberately set both "business-as-usual goals" and parallel and distinct stretch intentions. Staff trained themselves to live in two different worlds at the same time. In the first, everyday world, they set predictable goals, did their jobs as best they could, and performed according to a historically sensible view of the future. Their lives were relatively comfortable; their view of the future, tinged with resignation; their budget, predictable.

In their other world, they played high-stakes poker:
- They set bold goals.
- They kept people on their toes through constant, explicit attention to their work and accomplishment.

- They insisted on commitment to short-term stretch results as a condition of membership in certain activities.
- They frequently referred to the grand, ethical purposes of the organization as the legitimate basis for extraordinary effort.
- They made partnership and personal counseling a way of life in the service of the organization's stretch goals.
- They introduced a performance management system that included the achievement of stretch goals.

Often the company achieved its stretch goals, and it led the industry in performance during a very difficult recession. At the same time, staff lived and worked in a stable universe where, most of the time, people respected each other and took the time to enjoy life and their colleagues.

Imagining Camelot Is More Important than Knowing It[14]

—Specify the Exact Culture Changes Wanted

My wife and I watch our six-year-old son, George, move on skis for the first time. Fifteen minutes later, we see Gary, the instructor, escort our boy to the ski lift, and our hearts quicken. They move down the mountain slowly, Gary skiing backwards, and George holding on to a ski pole suspended horizontally in front of him. Gary then moves beside George, continuing to hold out his ski pole for the confidence and stability it provides. Near the bottom of the hill, Gary eases back slightly to George's rear and releases the ski pole. George, thinking his mentor is still by his side, still holds on to the pole—but skis down the rest of the way by himself.

Gary had opened for George a confident future as a skier. George now felt in his body and saw in his mind what it was like to conquer

---

[14]A spinoff from Einstein's statement that "Imagination is more important than knowledge" (*On Science*).

a steep, snowy mountain and knows he can do so. He will ski again. Minutes before his lesson, I helped George put on his skis and tried to teach him how to move forward and climb a small hill. As a ski mentor, however, I was a disaster. I had no clear idea what I was doing, or where my "instruction" was going. The dismaying result was that we both wanted to quit. Minutes later, helped by someone with the future precisely in mind, George was skiing—competently and happily.

What almost happened when I—a loving father but an inept ski instructor—tried to help George learn to ski happens all too often in companies trying to change the way they operate. As George needed Gary in this instance, Arthur often needs Merlin to guide him in pulling Excalibur from the stone. Often, without the guidance of a mentor, companies either fail to be specific about the exact culture changes they want, or they don't create exit criteria that allow them to acknowledge success or confront failure as the change effort proceeds.

Aligning for Change

One company's senior team developed a fine set of alignments for culture change that encompassed what they wanted both for their own team and for the organization as a whole. Each leader ultimately signed the following statement:

1. I will be personally responsible for making the senior team a paradigm for all corporate interaction; thus, partnership and quality will become the way of life in this group and throughout the company.
2. I am committed to open, honest, and precise communication that empowers all of us in common conversation. Thus, I will:
   - turn complaints into powerful requests for action and will see that they are addressed to someone who can act.
   - not speak or act in a manner that disempowers anyone in the organization.
   - raise issues directly with others.
   - speak freely, constructively, and directly.
3. I will point out perceived problems and seek support in appropriate action to correct them.

4. I will keep all possible options open in my discussions and in my relationships.

5. I will recognize people throughout the company for their contributions and accomplishments, and I acknowledge that we are all responsible, directly and indirectly, for each others' successes and failures.

6. I will be action-oriented and organized in meeting my commitments: I will:

   - be on time and prepared for all scheduled meetings, phone calls, and other commitments or acknowledge unkept promises.

   - open meetings with a statement of purpose and intended results; establish an agenda; make responsible assessments; set time limits; and end meetings with a clear understanding of what the next steps should be and who is responsible for taking them.

7. When others are speaking, I will listen to what they have to say from their point of view.

8. I will make no commitments or requests that I have no intention of fulfilling.

9. I will penetrate with "why questions"[15] all important business discussions, and I will never superficially address the well-being of this business as a business.

   By endorsing this document, I affirm these cultural principles as my own.

For at least two years, this company experienced a significant culture change. Many of these agreements were honored, and the effects radiated to many other parts of the company. As in much human endeavor, however, eventually the leaders, wearied of repetitive progress reviews and distracted by their own career and control concerns, became unwilling to spend the time needed to move to the next phase of culture change.

Members of this senior team did well to specify the exact culture they wanted. Change faltered, however, when they failed to sustain

---

[15]That is, executives agreed to ask why until they reached the root cause of problems.

the vision of their desired future, giving a corporate example of the truth of golf master Jack Nicklaus's statement that 50 percent of a great game is imaging, 40 percent is setup, and 10 percent is in the swing. As in golf, corporate culture change is continuous: Unless all-important vision, preparation, and action are in constant play, the game deteriorates quickly.

DEMAND A ROUND TABLE

—REQUIRE TEAM PLAY

Said the vice president of a pharmaceutical company,

> For most of my life, I've loved stars. I have a mental collection of them—from baseball, football, basketball, the movies, politics, and the military. The star system, therefore, seemed to me the right way to run a company, and I looked for and rewarded heroic figures who produced dramatic results. For years, as I tried to operate the company with stars, I couldn't understand why everyone didn't like my approach.
>
> After all, there was lots of applause. I enjoyed the drama and excitement. Who needed team play? It turned out that we did. I came to see that we rarely fulfilled our responsibilities when work required coordinated activity from groups of people.
>
> For that, the culture of our company would have to change.

What this executive had failed to notice was that baseball, football, and basketball players make up *teams*. An army pulls together or is decimated. A politician needs her staff and constituents, and a film star needs director, script, costume designer, other actors, and so forth.

Deliberate, aligned culture change doesn't happen without absolute leadership commitment to the team play that is prerequisite to a Round Table. While rhetoric and literature inevitably favor organizational teamwork, actual team play is comparatively infrequent.

Cooperative action requires focused attention, energy, and invented process to create and sustain. Even when the charge to join together sounds, most leaders lean more toward rewarding individual performances than team efforts.

This is understandable. The United States and much of the industrialized world espouse a culture of individualism. Our heroes and heroines tend to be solo figures, and we tend to acknowledge individuals rather than groups. Teams often develop to solve problems, not because of belief in the quintessential virtue of the team process. The deepest commitment is to the individual, who is really seen as the source of significant results.

A friend of mine believes that 10 percent of the people do everything, and she has lots of evidence for her conclusion. As a child, she decided she was not a team player and that, whenever pressed, she would act alone. My friend is rare in that she doesn't even pretend that teams are a good idea. One client is more typical. He champions teams as the best way to run his company, but he acts alone.

Culture change happens when people alter the ways they relate to each other. Particular adjustments occur in the relationships between bosses and their subordinates and among people with fundamentally different procedural or political interests. But greater partnership risks upsetting existing agreements and ways of operating, and most leaders would, like Melville's Bartleby the Scrivener, "prefer not to."

⟞

Follow Your Heart

—Lead Process Change from Commitment Change

In Arthurian terms, change the prize, not just the quest. My world has become process happy. "Methods improvement," "redesign," "reengineering," and so forth, are routine parts of all organization developers' vocabularies. I know process improvement is widespread, because some people now say it doesn't actually exist. Russell Lincoln Ackoff (1994) argues cogently that the idea of continuous improvement is fallacious and that meaningful change is, by its very nature, a discontinuity or a breakthrough. The informed speculation of paleontologist Stephen Jay Gould and others that evolution proceeds through sudden and drastic rather than gradual change offers a geologic parallel to Ackoff's belief. Evolution, far from being expressed as an orderly linear ladder "leading predictably to the evolution of consciousness" (1985b, p. 430) comprises instead quirky, explosive mass extinctions, which "may be the primary and indispensable seed of major changes and shifts in life's history" (1985a, p. 449). In fact, humankind may owe its existence to the comet now thought by many to have extinguished the dominant dinosaurs.

Many management consultants say that attempts to change organizations by changing process usually fail because this approach does not eliminate cultural roadblocks. What I observe is that any fundamental improvement happens in a looking-glass world, where facts turn quickly into opinions and unspoken commitments are quiet saboteurs.

Consider that there is no process change without commitment change and that, when people try new methods without altering their fundamental commitments, not much really happens. Consider also that a process is never more than a physical Glastonbury reflection of a commitment. When people's primary attention is paid to the means rather than the ends, the commitment generating the process dilutes. Rigid bureaucracies are an example.

Alterations in process are achieved more easily than changes in commitment, which may, in some instances, be immovable. Much serious cost cutting, for example, is performed by outsiders who don't share the concerns of the people affected inside. On the other hand, commitment rarely exists in a vacuum; it usually nests in a background of fears and concerns about possibilities. And often, when people expand their sense of the possible and transcend their fears, they find themselves committed to a previously unthinkable goal. In those moments, people often find that they were committed to that end in the first place without knowing it.

To change and sustain a culture, critical and supportive processes must transform to be consistent with the desired future. Only leadership's conviction that effective process change reflects commitment change makes such a metamorphosis possible.

⇌

FACE THE DRAGON

—TAKE ON WHAT YOU WOULD AVOID

People who really want to change a culture must keep taking on what they would rather avoid. This catch-all principle takes almost all organizations up a notch, because whatever they avoided has been forbidden. State the taboo openly, or ask about it. With practice, what is forbidden in any situation will be clear after just a few minutes.

The Cost of Retreat

Many people don't even realize they are avoiding. For example, certain individuals keep reenrolling in self-development groups. In every seminar of a long series, such recidivists demonstrate the entry behavior they had taken to their last experience. Some arrive shy; some, aggressive; some, careful; some, bold. After a while, they settle down, become at ease, interact naturally, have a few insights, and go home. Typically, the returnees feel that they have had such a great experience that they would often appear at subsequent seminars, but they rarely learned anything life-altering because they never confronted what they were avoiding. Companies without the courage to face what they fear often turn to consultant after consultant and buy program after program only to suffer the same momentarily uplifting but ultimately irrelevant consequences.

In the past few years, I've seen companies successfully avoid:
- ❧ telling the truth to their owners.
- ❧ confronting the fact that a vice president throws tantrums.
- ❧ dealing with conflicts among divisions or in other groups.
- ❧ recognizing misalignment between the human resource division and line management.
- ❧ reaching decisions about anything important.

When people avoid what scares them, although the usually widely known secret remains unspoken, it becomes an important part of the culture. *What is unsaid steers the corporate ship.* Like the courtiers who refused to admit that the emperor was naked, people are often unwilling or unable to tell the story of their modern corporate bureaucracy honestly.

The chief executive officer of one company grew up in a family where everyone bickered at the dinner table. He learned that, if he kept his mouth shut, either one of his brothers would defeat the others, or his parents would shush them and reward him with praise or some small privilege. This pattern, which seemed to have worked so well when he was a boy, became his way of managing all conflicts in life. By watching and letting others work problems out, he became head of a famous company and a community leader.

Unfortunately, his management system set limits for others. Disputes that could only be solved at his level were never addressed. Critical cost-reduction activity and process reengineering stalled at the boundaries of departments because of the missing forum from which the company could be seen as a whole. Only the chief executive officer could call such meetings and assure the presence of key people. His childhood fear of conflict was writ large on the lives of thousands of employees and millions of customers.

The limits of his personal universe would be the limits of the company's horizon until he learned the importance of dealing with what he avoided.

The Courage to Be[16]

Gradually, he became able to name to himself what he feared, confront it, and set a goal that forced him to stand in the face of what he would avoid. This process, while certainly neither easy nor pleasant, produces an unlikely and usually satisfying success.

---

[16]The title of Paul Tillich's important philosophical statement (1952/1959). "Courage," writes Tillich, "is self-affirmation 'in spite of,' that is in spite of that which tends to prevent the self from affirming itself" (p. 32). Tillich distinguishes usefully between anxiety and fear; the latter is "an object and makes participation possible . . . . Love in the sense of participation can conquer fear" (p. 36). Action is not possible against *anxiety*, however, unless it can be transformed into fear: "But ultimately, the attempts to transform anxiety into fear are vain. The basic anxiety, the anxiety of a finite being about the threat of nonbeing, cannot be eliminated. It belongs to existence itself" (p. 39).

So the best we can do is muster the courage to be in spite of.

5 THE GATEWAYS

AD 585

Arthur stood at the pinnacle of the "Tor"—the pointed magic mountain on the holy Isle of Avalon rising above the Glastonbury plain. Surrounded by marsh, this city of priestesses would become his final resting place.

Suddenly, inexplicably, poised between the visible order below and the evanescent myths shaping his quest, Arthur looked into the center of the Universe, the hiding place of the Holy Grail. He stood there between Glastonbury and Avalon.

AD 1994

Players talk about going into the zone; when the ball seems to move in slow motion. You don't realize it's happening until usually after a game. You sit back and think about plays, and all of a sudden it feels as if that line parts, and you can see the whole field, almost directly to your sides through your peripheral vision. All the vision that you want. Sometimes it happens that way, and other times there are just a lot of people in front of you.

—*Joe Montana*
Quarterback

rthur's Tor and Joe Montana's zone are gateways between Glastonbury and Avalon. In these passages, the mind moves outside of usual constraints. Traversing the gateways changes the ways people relate to one another. In the gateways, aborigines reach into dream time; there, for a moment, life becomes a work of art; there, the uncatchable pass is snagged; there, the impossible dream, dreamed.

At gateways in the corporate world, senior managers aspire to perform far beyond what is expected. At gateways, a company ignites in shared vision and collective responsibility. At gateways, people engage in a particular way of acting, talking, listening, and focusing attention that bridges the material and the relational. The gateways are design elements of an aligned organization poised for business success. If they stay closed, history is likely to repeat itself.

Gateways give a leader access to the undivided whole, to Camelot, which comprises both Glastonbury and Avalon, and where personal and collective quests are real. Camelot happens when preference for Avalon or Glastonbury disappears into a balance between attention to structure and process and to relation and flexibility. Both places continue to exist as separate entities; Arthur and the knights, however, reach Camelot when they commit simultaneously to both worlds while sustaining the ability to summon up what is necessary from either at any point. The paradoxical whole that is Camelot consists of suspended dichotomies, balanced scales. There is no day without night on earth, and there is no Glastonbury without Avalon in the corporate sphere—or at least, not for long.

Through gateways, companies can, for a moment, leave chronological, linear time and enter the timeless world of future, spirit, and possibility. Through gateways, companies can heal their past, enjoy their present, and face the unpredictable future with confidence.

The gateway experience can be dramatic. So, for me, was walking in a Western arroyo, a winding dry river bed, a narrow, rock-strewn, sandy path. In the hills of northern New Mexico, I followed one for miles. As I followed its twists and turns—walking in the path the river had cut aeons earlier—I passed mountains, hawks, prairie dogs, flowers. I walked without conscious purpose or distraction, letting sights, sounds, smells block out incessant criticism and unchosen circumstances. Each moment in the *arroyo* was present and total, intact and distinct, pulling me toward the future as it fulfilled its meandering intent. In this experience is the essence of a gateway between Glastonbury and Avalon, as perfect presence and perfect intent combine.

A gateway can change a scattered group into an aligned whole, can move people from criticism to affirmation, can shift individualists into partners, can change employees who see themselves as victims into responsible members of an organizational team. A gateway can turn resignation into confidence that "we" can handle anything together. A passage through a gateway, which leads to the culture change that opens a new business future, is remembered and sought again and again. At the gateways, corporate revitalization happens.

Yoga comprises over 50,000 positions. While there are at least as many gateways between corporate Glastonbury and Avalon, passage through the five discussed below have proven especially useful in helping organizations strive to revitalize, transform their cultures, and make widespread commitments to results. These arching gateways are:
- committing to another's success.
- starting in the future.
- coinventing.
- listening generously.
- speaking the truth of the heart.

When leaders consciously take on improving particular relationships, progress is usually remarkable. When they don't, progress stumbles. The question is, which relationships are leaders committed to and which are simply instrumental?

In complex organizations involving many sites and thousands of people, senior managers are often primarily concerned with improving the way they relate to each other, and to their superiors, and to their direct superiors. In these cases, developing the rest of the organization is often relegated to mere "training" rather than attention to essential relationships. Often, middle managers and workers are viewed as tools to use, rather than hearts and minds to win and share. According to this logic, development monies are mostly spent teaching "skills" to the lower ranks and providing them with the information they need to do their jobs. Even team effectiveness is construed as a skill, rather than a relational issue. Without committed relationships knitting together the whole system, most people are unwilling to undergo the stress and pay the concerted attention necessary to generate change.

MOVING BETWEEN THE REALMS

Committing to Another's Success

If I am not for myself, who am I?
If I am not for others, what am I?
If not now, when?

—*Rabbi Hillel (1st century BCE)*[17]

Over a decade ago, during our first meeting in Vienna, Virginia, financial advisor Jacques Rebibo offered to commit to my prosperity

---

[17]That is, first century before the Christian Era.

if I promised to take *his* advice. Until then, no one had ever been so explicitly committed to my success. I accepted his offer, and we built a solid partnership that contributed greatly to my financial well being. Rebibo, who proved to be even more faithful to my financial goals than was I, made many successful decisions on my behalf that I would not have had the knowledge to make myself. This agreement was my first conscious experience with committing to another's success. And I owe more to Rebibo than money—over the years, I have discovered that this connection was a primary gateway into the magical combination of hard results and uncommon relationship.

In contrast, during a planning retreat for Forensic Technologies International (which studies accidents and provides expert testimony), Chief Executive Officer Dan Luczak told his leadership team he believed that everyone in the Maryland-based company was totally in the grip of self-interest or a "for me" paradigm. And Luczak was right. We *all* live in a "for me" world. Normally, self-interest affects how we analyze data and determines what motivates us.

"This is natural," he admitted. "I do too. And we can all stay stuck in this crippling game, if that's what we really want. But consider—there are other alternatives."

As the group talked about life in the grip of self-interest, individuals began to recognize the power "for me" thinking had over them. They described how it expressed itself in their thinking about their own careers and how clearly it came out—now that they had a name for it—in their view of their own departments, their own turf, their own points of view, and their own way of doing things. As they talked, enthusiasm and new ideas began almost to explode "like a revolution," in the words of one executive. They discussed new ways to diversify, new ways to expand their offerings, and new ways to market their products.

At this point, Luczak said, he decided to start *acting* as if he were the chief executive officer of a $50 million company, even though, at the moment, the organization was grossing $8 million. His new point of

view and behavior changed the reality of his surroundings, and, shortly after his decision, ignition began. Over the following three years,
Forensic Technologies International tripled its business.

In committing to others' success in a particular arena, partners
begin, naturally, to discover what their fellows want personally, in
terms of accountability, and for the company as a whole. If the main
reason for a relationship is to help the other person win, then pro-
moting one's own views and opinions becomes irrelevant. When people in a company realize they can succeed by being deeply committed to others' progress, the context of the company itself shifts from
self-interest to cooperation.

This is not the usual condition either in most of the animal kingdom
or in the business world. Usually, people think and act out of self-
interest. In conflict, typically the best they do is to practice interest-
based negotiation, which is often adequate to the situation but insufficient to produce cultural transformation and a fundamental shift in
operation.

The practice of committing to the success of others and then supporting them over time provides the framework for the communication, conflict resolution, and cross-functional problem penetration
that lead to organizational change. In one company, my commitment
to the president's success keeps opening doors that would otherwise
close in the face of his arbitrary and authoritarian control of management and development processes. When I look at him through spontaneous eyes, my opinions and judgments make me want to flee; in
response, he brags and hides his problems. When I recommit to his
success, he begins to listen, there is usually some opportunity to contribute, and he is grateful. Committing to someone else's success is not
a technique with simple steps: It's a shift in point of view and intention. It is simple—and difficult.

Allan Sutherland, president and chief operating officer of the
Toronto-based Derlan Industries, Specialty Products Division, heads
12 business units within his organization.

He wrote,

> Before I met you, I was Mr. Nice Guy. I liked to be liked by everyone, and that kept me from being "unreasonable." I'm a lot better now, because I am willing to act in the context of the needs of the other 12 presidents' commitments for success, a context I now share. I've been unwavering in my commitment to their commitments for new products and markets, because that is one of the keys to our future. So we've been conscientiously looking to accelerate the rate of market and product development in the face of short-term demands. I think that my relationships with the other presidents have strengthened immeasurably; I am supportive of what they're trying to do, but I also keep trying to raise expectations. My role as a coach is to set high expectations on their behalf. When entrepreneurs start a business, they make a huge commitment toward what's possible. It's clear to me that advances in human endeavor, be it in business or elsewhere, happen because people make commitments. My inevitable reasonableness got in the way of such commitment, especially when it involved expectations that other people would act. That unreasonable reasonableness is gone.

I remember the moment, early in a session to define strategic vision, when I told a chief executive officer I would be more committed to what he wanted than was he. In that instant, we walked through the gateway. His eyes cleared, and he said, "Yes, and if we can all make the same promises among ourselves here, we can heal the heart of our business and culture." As I accepted his commitment as if it had been my own, his pledge to the success of his subordinates took them together into Avalon, and they began to work together in both domains in ways they had never experienced.

Starting in the Future

"I want to fly like that," Jonathan said, and a strange light glowed in his eyes. "Tell me what to do." Chiang spoke slowly and watched the younger gull ever so carefully. "To fly as fast as

thought, to anywhere that is," he said, "you must begin by knowing that you have already arrived."

—*Richard Bach*
Jonathan Livingston Seagull (*1970*)

T. H. White writes in *The Once and Future King* of Merlin's ability to
know the future. At one point, the king's mentor explains how he can
foretell the future:

"Ah yes," Merlin said. "How did I know to set breakfast for two?
Now ordinary people are born forwards in Time, if you understand
what I mean, and nearly everything in the world goes forward too.
This makes it quite easy for ordinary people to live, but unfortunately I was born at the wrong end of time, and I have to live backwards from in front, while surrounded by a lot of people living forward from behind." (1965, p. 35)

While others could recall the past, Merlin's ability to remember the
future gave meaning to what was happening in the present in the context of what he knew would happen later. And, once Merlin introduced Arthur to the idea of starting in the future, the king developed
a special relationship to time. Like the magician, he learned to live in
the future.

In 1990, when Charles. S. Trefrey[18] was president of the National
Wholesale Druggists Association, he spoke out against an industry-
wide problem. Industry sales had grown consistently, and wholesale
druggists effectively applied technology to improve their productivity. Nonetheless, profit margins still declined, and a third of the association's members either sold out to large competitors or went out of
business altogether. The future promised more of the same, and most
individual captains were too busy trying to keep their personal ships
afloat to worry about the seaworthiness of the industry as a whole. As
association president and titular head of the industry, however, it was

---

[18]Trefrey is currently president of Breakthrough Conversations (Annapolis, Maryland).

Trefrey's job to do so. Luckily he was up to the charge and could imagine a future in which the industry prospered.

In the industrial future Trefrey envisioned, the entire pharmaceutical conglomerate—from manufacturing, to wholesale distribution, to information dissemination and retail distribution to physicians, hospitals, and drug stores—operated as one electronic web connected by information technology. Intense adversarial relationships between wholesalers and manufacturers would be rare, and pathways toward partnerships, well travelled. When Trefrey spoke of the future, it was with this industry model in mind, but his vision was so disconnected from most people's reality that they could not listen to him. Today, the wholesale drug industry has built the information system that was born in Trefrey's imagined future.

As Arthur, Trefrey listened and spoke from a future revealed by vision, imagination, and intention. He knew that when people live toward the future, their spirits are uplifted. Association members—buyers and sellers—who affirmed his vision, he believed, would be far more able to cooperate and pull together in the present than people and companies looking to separate futures, even if all were pleased with their unique images.

Trefrey saw association members as able to embrace a future disconnected from the limits and possibilities of today's world. He therefore gathered 120 wholesale drug industry executives together in Chicago to live for three days in a future that hitherto had existed only in Trefrey's mind. At the end of the retreat, which involved the telling of difficult truths, many shared the future Trefrey had imagined and began to create prosperous partnerships through electronic information exchange. With its people starting in the future, neither the industry as a whole nor their specific companies looked as if they were made up merely of bricks and mortar; they now seemed to comprise gentler materials that were malleable in a way they had not been moments before. Almost no one could explain what had happened, but suddenly a series of cooperative and productive agreements existed between people who, in former buyer-seller relationships, had been sure they could take no risks with one another.

"Drug wholesalers are now willing and able to use the power of their minds to create their future," Trefrey summarized. As Merlin committed himself to Arthur's future for Britain, Trefrey did the same for the members of his association. He prophesied it, invented it, and brought industry's kings together to make it real.

Coinventing

Perhaps you will recall that, when we disengaged last year, it was because we felt ready to ascend the steep slope in front of us and had established a new project that the team wanted to make happen. We have now just closed off the financial year, and I thought you would like to hear that we scaled a few peaks.

The challenge we have set for ourselves in 1994 is beyond what the previous plan showed for 1997. The point in all this is to say thank you for what you have done for the Perkins' international team. We have benefitted enormously from working with you. What's sure is that the job isn't done yet.

I'm looking forward to working with you again sometime in the future.

Best Regards,
Allan Arnott
Managing Director
Perkins International Limited
Peterborough, England

The thrust of Allan Arnott's letter, while apparently aimed only at Glastonbury, also reflects Avalon. Without the spirit of Avalon, the unpredictable rush to Perkins's goals Arnott describes could not have happened.

As much as anyone I have known, Allan Arnott uses his direct and extended teams to coinvent the future, a process that almost any group can accomplish as long as no one person controls it. For example, a group may coinvent vision, strategic intent, projects, goals, values, and fundamental ways of operating. When coinventing, the group may start from scratch, or it may build on a system or structure already in existence, in which case the original may be presented for critique, review, and improvement. Coinvention may initiate anywhere in the corporation—with senior executives, with middle managers, and/or with specialized or cross-functional groups. After leaders develop a vision or plan, they can present their view to other groups and work until everyone involved shares a commitment to the desired outcome.

Arnott trusts coinvention as an effective counter to the natural urge to control. Like other gateways, it has choice at its core. Arnott has taught me that, over time, the most effective control happens through alignment. At Perkins, coinvention has proven to be an ongoing process—a series of choices. Coinvention assumes that people are more likely to put their minds, hearts, and effort into something they have been part of creating than something that is presented as a *fait accompli*.

Often, people *feel* ordered and dominated if they have simply been *asked*. Through coinvention, however, the vision or plan is seen as neither "my idea" nor "yours," but something "we" own. Even if the idea originated with one person, coinvention levels the playing field, and it becomes "our idea." This gateway stays open, however, only when the leader stands firm for coinvention, even in the face of the pressing desire to proceed with what s/he thinks is right.

To coinvent requires that all in a group intend to inquire, talk, and speculate. These processes can happen only when the questions are not presumed to have answers foretold. Even if preliminary answers and solutions have already been worked out, *coinvention requires suspension of presumptions*. It does not require denial of previous thoughts, which may be proposed to the group. It does, however, insist that no one assumes s/he has the right answer. Coinvention involves engagement with others in the shared willingness to dwell in the unknown.

At any moment, during coinvention, participants can attend either to their certainty or their confusion about what is going on. Attending to one's confusion rather than to one's certainty allows true inquiry, dialogue, and speculation, and opens the gateway. Coinvention requires one to engage innocently and vulnerably, whether with 1 or 100 people, and to maintain the tone and substance of a genuine dialogue. It aims to create a stream of meaning within, among, and through the participants. Coinvention occurs when it is organizational leaders' primary intent. Much of the time, however, their goal is instead to prove themselves right about a decision already made, in order to look good, to feel safe, to minimize risk, and to keep the situation under control.

Most people do not coinvent. They arrive at meetings with the conviction that they have the solution already in their pocket, and they seek answers to the problem that will stack up to support their preexisting notions. If the leaders' intention to coinvent fails, meetings often become an endless contest of opinions in a fruitless search for agreement. Although issues are thrashed out and discussed, no one changes his or her mind or deeply held beliefs. Such a meeting can become an exercise in laboring to change people who refuse to budge.

While the wish to avoid danger and provide security are normal human tendencies, they must be overcome, if not eliminated, by a dedication to alignment or shared intention in the group. When the leaders' intent is to coinvent, the rewards can be substantial, as people give each other the benefit of the doubt, acknowledge the others' contributions, and imagine together creatively.

Listening Generously

I think, too often we hear possibilities in the context of who speaks them. I want a culture where people really listen to what others have to say. In a sense, the problem is like racism. People rarely admit to being racist, and executives usually insist that they listen to their employees. But in reality, noncommunication is the state in which most people exist.

If they can learn to listen generously, I'm sure, extraordinary performance will come out of ordinary people.

—*Allan R. Sutherland*
President and Chief Operating Officer
Specialty Manufacturing Group
Derlan Industries Limited
Toronto, Ontario, Canada

The truth is that I listen generously at work when I am committed to the person or group I'm helping or to the piece of work I'm doing. (As a consultant, I'm paid to listen; when I don't, I'm apt to lose my job.) If I am unable to commit, I've learned not to accept work offers: The result is tedious and unproductive for both the client and me.

But looking at my life as a whole, I don't listen generously very much, and a lot of the time I don't listen at all. It's become a kind of family joke. My daughters often address "Charlie" rather than "Dad," when they really want me to hear something, and my wife has learned to wait until I am in a good mood and wide awake before telling me anything important. I sometimes get upset and respond vigorously to something that was never said. So, as I write about the importance of generous listening, I feel hypocritical, knowing I'm likely to continue not practicing what I preach. The sports maxim is often true, however: The best coach isn't always the best player.

Nonetheless, every time executives see generous listening actually happening in a business-as-usual, turf-conscious culture, they open themselves up to a future they never thought possible. The difficulties we all have in listening generously and the inconsistent ways we often do so do not diminish its reality as one of the most hopeful acts I know.

Lew Epstein, a friend, teacher, and family counselor, defines compassion as the conscious concern for another human being. Through his life experience and his gifted spirit, Epstein has raised compassionate listening to an art, helping thousands of individuals, couples, and groups operate at a level of effectiveness they never thought was possible.

These days, when I find it hard to listen generously, I sometimes think of Epstein and attempt to copy his techniques. Remembering him, I offer care rather than severity in my attentiveness, and I become more willing to risk. To listen generously is to listen with deep appreciation of the feelings and point of view of the other person. It is a gateway between Glastonbury and Avalon and the undivided whole from which they both come.

Joseph Rael recounts the place generous listening holds in Native American tradition: "Listening is sensitivity. The true listener is no longer defined by desires or attachments. Instead he or she is sensitized to consciousness" (with Elizabeth Marlow, 1993, p. 67). Such listening is "sensitivity to all forms." Listening generously happens *only* when one intends to *appreciate* rather than to understand, evaluate, or use. It's not the same as being nice to people no matter what (although some of that isn't a bad idea). One can listen generously and respond directly. As one executive said, "I used to think that listening generously meant sitting quietly, interminably, with a little smile on my face. . . . I learned, however, that it does not mean withholding my own truth."

Generous listening is a way to create a social reality different from the one already there. In this sense, it is a doorway to a future that is not determined by the past. Whenever Arthur or the knights will not or cannot listen to each other generously, effective growth halts. Similarly, employees will resist what they cannot hear. To illustrate: For years, I have been trying to get one company president to hear that his own lack of cooperativeness is at the heart of his union problems, worker strikes, supplier problems, interdepartmental conflicts, managerial difficulties, and resistance to his program.

One day on the phone, I decided to just listen to him and his concerns. I asked him why he thought the employees listened to the union stewards and not to managers.

He answered, "They don't think we're trustworthy."
"Are you?" I asked.
"No," he said. "I guess not."

For once, I had stopped trying to steer the conversation so it would end up with him accepting my point of view. As soon as *I* began listening generously instead of trying to fix him, his arrogance disappeared, and *he* found his own answer.

By their own report, people in companies listen poorly to one another. Once people get a taste of generous listening, they experience its power and effectiveness. Yet, as a single technique to get work done and deal with people more effectively, generous listening can lose its power. After a while, they come to find the practice difficult and not always successful. Then, they justify their failure to listen generously in the face of constant pressure to act and produce. Finally, they stop practicing and resent "another management technique that doesn't work." Rather than take pleasure in the discipline of listening generously while overcoming increasingly higher obstacles, they give it up and look elsewhere for help.

Still, I have seen generous listening enable progress in hundreds of large and small groups. When leaders are being vulnerable, when they let their own humanity be seen in public, when they don't have all their answers already assembled, the outcome almost always includes a new sense of partnership and high-performance commitments. And generous listening begets both more generous listening and generous responses in return. This widening circle opens when people continue to listen generously in the face of disagreement, resistance, anger, upset, urgency, and strong opinion. The challenge to leadership is to put aside their reactions and opinions and to rise above themselves over and over again. It calls them to renew their commitment to the people to whom they are listening, and the experience can be awkward, emotional, and risky.

Sometimes, generous listening involves learning to listen for the contribution and commitment in others' words rather than hearing one's own inner assessments, opinions, and judgments of those words. Too often, we think we already know what the other person is going to say. We are not even present to the words of the speaker. Generous listening asks us to suspend our judgment about what is being said until the speaker is finished, and the wait is often difficult. At these times, I remember that Glastonbury without Avalon is a sterile place.

Shortly after a recent conference during which we had explored generous listening, the owner of a midwestern industrial supply distributor wrote to his 10-year-old son. Excerpted here, the letter captures the essence of generous listening.

Dear Alex,

When you get home I'll tell you all about it, but right now I want to tell you some of the things I've learned that are going to make me the greatest dad in the world. (I know you think I already am the best, but I've learned some secrets that will make me even a better one.)

You know how we always seem to talk, over and over again, about your needing to do certain things, or how I get angry and yell at you about the same things all the time? And then sometimes we both get real mad at each other? Well, that's going to stop, because I've learned in this school that I can really make it stop if I want to, and I really want to. You see, it's just a bad habit I have that I need to change. And they're teaching me ways to change those habits. You know how? By listening to what you have to say and then talking with you about why you said it. You know how you sometimes tell Mom that I don't listen to you or let you talk? Well, you were right! That doesn't mean you'll always be right, or that I'll agree with you, but I will respect what you have to say, and then we'll talk with each other about it.

And you know how you tell Mom you can't talk to me about some things, because you think I'll be angry with you, or you already know how I'll act or what I'm going to say? Guess what? That's another bad habit I'm getting rid of. I want you to know that I really care about anything you feel a need to share with me and that I'm ready to listen to you.

We both know that sometimes things aren't so good between us. Well, one of the most important secrets I've learned here is that I'm the one responsible for it not being so good. It's not your fault; it's mine. You know how I've taught you to stand up and take the blame when you screw up? Well, I'm taking the blame for this one, buddy.

See you in less than a week.

Love,
Dad

Thus, generous listening works in both personal and corporate spheres. Over and over, I've seen great companies in trouble change their future by establishing generous listening as a core value and committing to its practice. It's important to remember, however, that generous listening remains a deliberate act, not a natural, instinctive, spontaneous one. It must be championed to become widespread and to be sustained.

The most culture change, demonstrated results, and sustainable progress I've seen has been in manufacturing plants where almost all of the people were involved together at one time. As they were able to hear each other's complaints, concerns, and dreams, something remarkable happened to their ability to seek and produce the extraordinary. As they came to accept the virtue of having a company in which people listen generously, were committed to each other's success, and started projects in the future, they leaped into action, and, as soon as the next day, the impossible had suddenly become practical. In the new, intact environment, with its clear boundaries, everyone entered the conversation at once.

Speaking the Truth From the Heart

Revitalizing an organization is not complex, specialized, or esoteric.

It's not rocket science. People simply forget—or maybe they never learned—the basic truths that keep commitment alive, relationships whole, and results a matter of fact. Even though I can usually list these truths, fear sometimes keeps me from remembering them. That fear also sometimes hampers Arthur and the knights.

Ten years ago, a friend of mine designed a genuinely new form of jewelry. On his way to getting rich from his invention, he began receiving calls from major companies threatening to produce his jewelry. If he protested, they said, they would litigate him into poverty. A gentle man who wished only to reap the rewards of his own invention, he went through a period of deep distress. Rivals did succeed in stealing his idea, and—although he finally recovered financially—the emotional cost was enormous. Though the pain is still a bitter memory, he has resumed his career as a successful and original jeweler and become a generous humanitarian as well.

Recently, as he and I were driving to a meeting, he recounted this story. In response, I offered to buy him a drink, an inappropriate gesture to a teetotaler, which I made knowing that he didn't drink. I felt shallow and awkward. He remained silent. About five minutes later, he asked, "Why did you say that?"

He had been honest with me, and I realized I had been afraid to say what was true for me. A moment later, I confessed, "I want to apologize to you for all those companies and lawyers who acted so blindly, hurt you so badly, and didn't even know or care that they were doing it. I am sorry they didn't take responsibility for what they did, and I apologize to you for them."

He received my apology in silence; then, a few more miles down the road, I saw tears on his cheeks. When he had composed himself, he told me that, when the jewelry companies had stolen his invention, he had retreated from everything to do with business. Now, after my apology, he said, he thought he could see a possibility of working with people in business again. He thanked me for helping him release his past.

Later, he asked why my first response had been so inappropriate. I said I had been afraid to face the part of me that I'd have to face in order to contribute to him. I saw that it was my fear of looking strange, not sounding conventional. He then asked where my apology came from. I said—and this is true—"it came out from out of nowhere."

Many peoples around the world have a ritual that helps them tell the truth to one another in important gatherings. In the Hawaiian tradition, the ritual is enacted by using a *paoa* or talking stick.[19] Those holding it speak the truth from their hearts, and everyone else listens. When people know they are safe and won't be interrupted, they gain the courage to speak their hearts' truth.

On occasion, I use the talking stick in my work with corporations. When it works, people quickly become authentic with one another, but only when the leadership is committed to an open, honest company is it effective. (The *paoa* has only failed me once, when the chief executive officer of a worldwide insurance conglomerate lied about his wish for honesty.) Here, as through all of the gateways, the magic happens only when the leader is genuinely committed to change. If the chief doesn't engage the process with conviction, neither will the team. For Merlin, such half-hearted engagement reliably identifies the pretender. In contrast, Arthur's commitment is total.

The *paoa* recently helped a British auto parts manufacturing leadership team to figure out how they could perform as exceptionally in the first three quarters of the year as they did in the fourth. They had been trying to do so without success for years. As the talking stick passed from person to person, the sensitivity and attentiveness in the room increased dramatically. Suddenly, someone pointed out,

You know that the top team spends 10 times as much time with us

---

[19]My gratitude again to Ross LewAllen, who first introduced me to the power of the talking stick. (See Acknowledgments.)

in the fourth quarter as they do in the rest of the year. Only then are we in full, good communication with the executives, and only then do we really know what others are dealing with.

The knight told the truth, and the company was on the road to new levels of performance. The actual conversation centered in Glastonbury: The talk was of engines, customers, cash flow, and technology. But the Avalon truth came from the heart. Operating in Glastonbury from Avalon consciousness, we built Camelot in an austere conference room in the Midlands of England.

On another occasion, we brought the talking stick to a meeting with the leadership team of a U.S. technology company that had lost its former preeminence. Seated in a crowded, tacky, narrow room, littered with stray wires and defunct computers, we heard a litany of corporate woes. Its markets were eroding. Smaller, more agile competitors with blood in their eyes were bringing innovative products to market faster than could be imagined. Friends and colleagues had already lost their jobs, and more cuts were on the way. The bureaucracy ruled; no one in the company felt powerful.

Opening the meeting with the talking stick felt risky. I had met with these people only once before, and they had a reputation for conservatism. Common practice says that real men and real business people never make themselves vulnerable in this way. Many people believe that speaking the truth from the heart is appropriate in personal life but not in business. We fear that such speaking threatens a loss of control and, by revealing private knowledge, gives away a secret weapon of corporate power.

Against this backdrop, I explained the rules: The person holding the *paoa* was to "speak the truth from the heart" about the business, uninterrupted. After explaining the place of the talking stick in ancient ritual, I noted that today's stick was exactly the same length as the tribal standard upon which a friend had modeled it. I had chosen the symbols and colors on the stick and each had a personal meaning. "My intent," I continued, is for you to heal the past and to speak to one another in a way that your hopes for your self and the company would come to pass. I'm excited to be working for a company with a great tradition and am humbled by the enormity of your challenge.

I passed the talking stick to the vice president who had brought the group together. Fed up with the backbiting, self-centered attitude his subordinates and colleagues brought to almost every important discussion, he had long expressed his frustration without being able to bring about the changes that would alleviate his company's difficulties. This meeting, he had said, "is to be *it* for me," explaining that unless first his division and then the company fundamentally changed the way they operated, he would leave. This vice president, who had been with the company for 25 years, loved the place. Because of that, he was putting himself, his reputation, and his future on the line.

He was Arthur, but Arthur with much to learn about unifying his kingdom and with many personal mountains to climb. Taking the stick and beginning to speak, the vice president summoned up his courage. Everyone listened in silence, and we found ourselves leaving that shabby Glastonbury room and entering Avalon. As others spoke, uninterrupted, any future began to seem possible.

The topics discussed usually bred defensiveness and resistance. "How will limited funds be allocated among departments for development?" "What products should we eliminate?" "Should we reorganize?" "Who should be in charge?" "How should we change the measurement system?"

This time, however, no one accused. Permission to speak the truth from the heart had produced forgiveness, apology, and healing, without disallowing the hard facts of business reality. With the truth telling came the peace of mind that arises when one is honest with oneself and other human beings.

We had disconnected mentally and emotionally from the past, and we had connected as a profoundly cohesive group. The "we versus they" climate disappeared. The talking stick and its symbolic commitment to honoring people's personal truth had demonstrated an age-old lesson: Sharing personal truth sets people free.

When only Glastonbury is real, speaking the truth from the heart can seem odd, inappropriate, irrelevant, and a sign of weakness. In some companies, the culture of Glastonbury is so strong that it takes rare courage, even for an outsider, to advocate telling the truth from the heart. Doing so, however, often cuts through business problems and barriers to change like a hot knife through butter.

Truth telling is a fierce act that removes men and women from the civility of modern corporate life and returns them to a time when honor, chivalry, and questing were expected. Like all of the gateways, it calls for choice, looks to the future, and heals the past.

⊬

THE TERRIBLE TRUTH

For months, ongoing high-level discussions at a computer-manufacturing company, employing 120,000 and grossing $3 billion annually, considered how to improve the measurement system for rewarding effective, outstanding employees. The talk was endless and fruitless. Again and again, the staff gathered together to come to closure about this measurement system. Hours later, the boss would call the meeting to a close, saying she would make a unilateral decision, which she never did.

I realized that the group could never agree on a reward system, because the corporate culture wouldn't let them. After attending several of their pointless meetings, I interrupted the bickering and asked the participants to stop sniping and tell the truth from their hearts.

"What's the terrible truth about what just happened here during the last hour?" I asked. The knights responded that the terrible truth was that:

* people don't really behave consistently with any measurement system.
* people keep blaming the measurement system as a way of keeping themselves from doing any cross-functional activity.
* this bickering has been going on for a year.
* people simply do what they want to do or like to do or are good at and they do what gets them acknowledgment.
* the measurement system has little impact on people's behavior or effectiveness, but we keep blaming it for our problems and have endless discussions about it.

The "terrible truth" is a form of speaking the truth from the heart that brings immediacy to a situation. It forces people out of the conceptual, observational mode of talking, into the arena of action. After each member of the group had said what was—for him or her—the terrible truth, they quickly reached consensus:

> The terrible truth is that we must choose a measurement system because the company requires it. No matter which one we choose, it will matter little to people in the organization. So we should stop talking about it, select one, and get on with life.

Which is what they did, in about 10 minutes.

On the surface, it seems as if going through the gateways has its major effect in Avalon, but this is not the case. When Arthur and the knights are willing to keep moving through the gateways, the process has dramatic effects on Glastonbury results as well.

CREATING THE GATEWAYS

Our challenge in defining gateways between the realms is to find innovative measures which, in themselves, lead to new, unified possibilities for people and performance. David Bohm (1980) recognizes the challenge of visualizing continuity, wondering, "How are we to think coherently of a single, unbroken, flowing actuality of existence as a whole . . . instead of . . . inherently divided, disconnected, and broken into yet smaller constituent parts?" (p. x). He quotes Kant's belief that all experience is organized according to categories of thought. Difficult as juggling such components is, however, the unity gained by achieving that task is worth a great deal. Bohm continues, "When the whole field of measure is open to original and creative insight without any fixed limits or barriers, then our overall world views will cease to be rigid" (p. 25).

Epilogue

Many successful consultants, chief executive officers, and senior executives often look and sound worn out. While they speak with pride about their companies, their dreams, and the energy they derive personally from their work, they project images of kings with uncertain futures. Sometimes, I see one as Arthur, dressed for yet another battle, to which s/he looks forward with confidence, hoping it will be the best . . . and last. Changing a company culture and the way it operates is a "hero's journey" (Joseph Campbell's phrase, 1988). Some knights balk and undermine the process. The limitations of the king and others will often seem so pervasive that change looks unlikely. And, as Amy Hertz points out, "only a grotesque amount of energy can sustain a system in which reality keeps punching holes" (1994, p. 14).

In these moments, one's partnerships, constancy of purpose, and sense of humor are all-important. In these moments, courage, clarity, and humanity clear chaos from the mind. *Lives* are at stake, and the struggle is worth the prize. In these moments, there are beginnings.

REFERENCES

Ackoff, Russell Lincoln. (1994). *The democratic corporation*. New York: Oxford University Press.

Allport, Gordon. (1970). *The nature of personality: Selected papers*. Westport, CT: Greenwood. (Original work published 1950)

Bach, Richard. (1970). *Jonathan Livingston Seagull*. New York: Macmillan.

Bateson, Gregory. (1972). *Steps to an ecology of mind*. New York: Ballantine

Barthelemy, Robert. (1994) *The sky is not the limit: Breakthrough leadership*. Dayton, OH: Author.

Baum, Neil. (1992, February 17). Doctors can learn much from Disney about patient visits. American Medical News, 35(7), 32.

Body Shop, The. (1995). *Retailing is wonderful for continuous reinvention: It's a crazy, complicated journey*. Watersmead, Littlehampton, West Sussex, England: Author.

Bodian, Stephen. (1993, November/December). An interview with Jack Kornfield. *Yoga Journal*, 113, 56.

Bohm, David. (1980). *Wholeness and the implicate order*. London: Ark.

Bradley, Marion Zimmer. (1982). *The mists of Avalon*. New York: Ballantine.

Buber, Martin. (1978). *I and thou*. (Walter Kaufman and S. G. Smith, Trans.) New York: Macmillan. (Original work published 1923)

Buber, Martin. (1965). *Between man and man*. (Ronald G. Smith, Trans.) New York: Macmillan. (Original work published 1947)

Campbell, Joseph (with Moyers, Bill). (1988). *The power of myth*. New York: Doubleday.

Catalyst. (1994). *The 1994 Catalyst census of female board directors of the Fortune 500/Service 500*. New York: Author.

Chopra, Deepak. (1994). *Ageless body, timeless mind: The quantum alternative to growing old*. New York: Crown.

Davis, W. Edwards. (1991). *Out of the crisis*. Cambridge, MA: Addison-Wesley.

Deming, Stanley M. (1990). *Future Perfect*. Redding, MA: Massachusetts Institute of Technology, Center for Advanced Engineering Study.

Dillard, Annie. (1982). *Teaching a stone to talk*. New York: Harper and Row.

Disney's recruiting and training program. (1992, 24 May), *Bakery Production and Marketing*, 27(5), 97.

Ditzler, Jinny S. (1994). *Your best year yet! A proven method for making the next 12 months your most successful ever.* London: Thorsons (HarperCollins).

Forster, E. M. (1981). *Howard's End.* Cutchogue, NY: Buccaneer. (Original work published 1910)

Gallwey, W. Timothy. (1974). *The inner game of tennis.* New York: Random House.

Gilchrist, Ellen. (1989). *Light can be both wave and particle.* Boston: Little Brown.

Gould, Stephen Jay. (1985a). Sex, drugs, disasters, and the extinction of dinosaurs. In *The flamingo's smile: Reflections in natural history* (pp. 417–426). New York: W. W. Norton.

Gould, Stephen Jay. (1985b). The cosmic dance of Siva. In *The flamingo's smile: Reflections in natural history* (pp. 438–450). New York: W. W. Norton.

Gould, Stephen Jay. (1991). The godfather of disaster. In *Bully for Brontosaurus: Reflections in natural history* (pp. 367–381). New York: W. W. Norton.

Hamel, Gary, and Prahalad, C. K. (1989, May/June). Strategic intent. *Harvard Business Review, 67*(3), 63–76.

Hertz, Amy. (1994, July/August). On sloth and other virtues. *Yoga Journal, 117,* 14–17.

Heschel, Abraham Joshua. (1955). *God in search of man.* New York: Noonday.

Hesse, Herman. (1963). *Steppenwolf.* (Basil Creighton, Trans.) New York: Modern Library. (Original work published in 1928)

King, Serge Kahili. (1990). *Urban shaman.* New York: Simon and Schuster.

Kuhn, T. S. (1970). *The structure of scientific revolutions* (2nd ed.). Chicago: University of Chicago Press.

Leonard, George. (1991). *Mastery.* New York: Penguin.

Lessons from Mickey Mouse: NASMD [National Association of Sheet Music Dealers] enrolls at Disney University to sharpen people skills. (1994, April). *The Music Trades, 142*(3), 58.

Levine, Stephen, and Levine, Ondrea. (1995, January/February). An experience in mystical unity. *Yoga Journal, 120,* 86.

Lewin, Kurt. (1951). *Field theory and social science.* New York: Harper.

Malory, Thomas. (1978). *Morte D'Arthur.* New York: Holmes and Meier. (Original work published 1485)

National Foundation for Women Business Owners and Dun and Bradstreet Information Services. (1995). *Breaking the boundaries—The progress and achievement of women-owned businesses.* Silver Spring, MD: National Foundation for Women Business Owners.

Oshry, Barry. (1977). *Power and Systems Training, Incorporated.* New Providence, NJ: Bowker.

Polster, Erving, and Polster, Miriam. (1973). *Gestalt therapy integrated.* New York: Brunner Mazel.

Redfield, James. (1994). *The Celestine prophesy.* New York: Warner Books.

Rael, Joseph (with Marlow, Elizabeth). (1993). *Being and vibration.* Tulsa, OK: Council Oak Books.

Riesman, David (with Glazer, Nathan and Denney, Reuel). (1969). *The lonely crowd: A study of the changing American character.* New Haven, CT: Yale University Press.

Rogers, Carl R. (1961). *On becoming a person.* Boston: Houghton-Mifflin.

Sartre, Jean-Paul. (1974). *Nausea.* New York: New Directions. (Original work published 1938)

Scott, Mary, and Rothman, Howard. (1992). *Companies With a Conscience: Intimate Portraits of Twelve Firms That Make a Difference.* New York: Birch Lane.

Steward, R. J., and Matthews, John (Eds.). (1995). *Merlin through the ages: A chronological anthology and sourcebook.* London: Blandford.

Stewart, Mary. (1980). *The crystal cave.* New York: William Morrow.

Thorsell, William. (1993, April 3). Mikhail Gorbachev: A reformer blown away by the winds of change. *Toronto Globe and Mail,* p. D6.

Tillich, Paul. (1959). *The courage to be.* New Haven: Yale University Press. (Original work published 1952)

Tolstoy, Nikolai. (1988). *The quest for Merlin.* Boston: Little Brown.

White, T. H. (1965). *The once and future king.* New York: G. P. Putnam.

Wilde, Stuart. (n.d.). *Camelot* (cassette recordings). Taos, NM: White Dove International.

Zukav, Gary. (1984). *The dancing Wu Li masters: An overview of the new physics.* New York: Bantam. (Original work published 1979)

ABOUT THE AUTHOR

Charles E. Smith, Ph.D., is an international management consultant helping organizations define their future and balanced pathways to it. Active in this field for over 25 years, Dr. Smith is currently a Director of Taos Laboratories, which researches and provides state of the art knowledge and technology for strategy, leadership, and partnership. Dr. Smith is a graduate of Boston Public Latin School, holds an A.B. from Harvard College, an M.B.A. from the Harvard Business School, and a Ph.D. in Organizational Behavior from Case Western reserve University. *The Merlin Factor* is his first book.